Hearing God

A 73-day devotional to help strengthen your connection to God

by

Ann Dee

ISBN:
eBook: 979-8-90224-116-4
Paperback: 979-8-90224-117-1
Hardback: 979-8-90224-118-8

Published by:
Authors Publishing House
178 Broadway, 3rd Floor, #1343
New York, NY 10001, USA

Main Line: (855) 624-0155
Email: support@authorspublishinghouse.com

Unless otherwise noted, Scripture quotations are taken from The Holy Bible, New International Version. Copyright 1978 by New York International Bible Society.

Published by Zondervan Corporation.

The Greek New Testament Copyright 2000 by Deutsche Bibelgesellschaft

Doitinhebrew.com

Table of Contents

Dedication

To God, Jesus, and Holy Spirit. Without you I am nothing.

To all the special pastors that helped me grow in Christ.

PB, R Salas, D Gabbard, JD Davis

Thank you, Gentlemen.

About The Author

A lifelong believer (and sinner) Ann Dee has always known Jesus. There was never an epiphany moment, He was always there. With a master's degree in theological studies from Southern Baptist Theological Seminary, Ann Dee has set out to spread the gospel in her writing and art. Ann Dee lives in Columbus, Ohio with her 5 cats. @andeha45 on Instagram

Introduction

There has never been a time in my life that I did not know Jesus. There were many times I ignored Him, but I always knew he was there. Probably with his arms crossed, tapping his foot.

I was raised in church and in that church were two people that helped shape me. They were my kindergarten Sunday school teachers. Mr. and Mrs. Arndt. They are with Jesus now but they were my biggest influences next to my parents. They were a part of my life until the day they died.

Mrs. Arndt sent me a devotional several years back that I read every day. One devotional a day for a year and it is wonderful. However, I thought a smaller one with key verses and my favorite verses would be powerful. A power to get those verses committed to your heart and soul. This devotion will not have verses in any particular order unless indicated. They are just my favorites.

The Bible is a library and can be read starting anywhere, so shall I. I will add something more depending on the verse. If it is Old Testament, I have added Hebrew and if New Testament, yes, Greek. I loved studying Hebrew and Greek at seminary. It opened up the world of that particular time.

As one pastor said to me, scripture knowledge is a tool we all need in our tool box. Even satan knows Scripture, lets know it better. We all need that tool to be a warrior for God.

This book is 73 days. Why 73 days, that's weird. Take 73 times 5 and you get 365. You go through this devotional 5 times a year. This will help get those verses in your heart and grow powerful.

The format is very simple. A verse, my commentary, a prayer and a space for your thoughts. Do reflect on the verses and commit them to your heart and soul. Praise be to God for his word.

Let the Holy Spirit speak to you each day. Look to Jesus as he smiles upon you. Open up to God's love.

Enjoy!

-ANN DEE

Day One

John 3:17

For God did not send his Son into the world to condemn the world, but to save the world through him.

*Greek**οὐ γὰρ ἀπὲστειλευ ὀ θεὸς τὸν υἱὸν εἰς τὸν κόσμου ἵνα κρίνῃῃ τὸν κόσμου, ἀλλ' ἵνα σωθῇ ὁ κόσμου δι ' αὐτοῦ.*

Although John 3:16 is the essence of Jesus, go a step further. Yet God sent His son to lead people to God but that is only part. Qualify that with this verse. God is not angry at us, he loves us. He sent Jesus not to smite but to open the vail to himself. Without the Son, no one sees the father. If it was in anger, no one would want to see the father. John 3:16 is passion and 3:17 is pure love.

Prayer**Your love, God, is amazing. A kind of love a mere human cannot comprehend. My finite and grateful heart cannot love you to the level of your love for me, but I will try. Thank you.

Your Thoughts…

Day Two

Matthew 27:46

About the ninth hour Jesus cried out in a loud voice, "Eloi, Eloi, lama sabachthani?"—which means, "My God, my God, why have you forsaken me?"

*Greek**περὶ δὲ τὴν ἐνάτην ὥραν ἀνεβόησεν ὁ Ἰησοῦς φωνῇ μεγάλῃ λέγων, Ηλι ηλι γεμα σαβαχθανι: τοῦτ' ἔστιν, Θεέ μου θεέ μου, ἱνατί με ἐγκατέλιπες:*

Have you ever been to a point where the pain is so great? How about a time when you felt completely alone. In this verse in Matthew and Mark, it is both. Jesus is in utter pain and loneliness. "Why father". I think the next words out of my mouth would be "sorry Dad" but Jesus knew his mission. He took the weight of all the sin past, present and future and to God he was hideous at that moment. God could not look at the love of his life and his creation in us. It was revolting. He turned away. Quickly it was over. Jesus died, took those hideous sins and descended to the depths of Hell. The deepest, darkest, loneliest place then deposited all that sin, our sins, where it all belongs. All the pain and loneliness we may experience will never ever compare to that moment when Jesus cried out for his dad. Our sin caused that ripple. Our sin is what is revolting, not us. Yet because Jesus proceeded to fulfill his mission, our stupid sin is where it belongs.

Prayer**Jesus, you suffered so great for me, a price I cannot repay. The only thing I can do is thank you and come closer to you every day of my life. My heart is full because of your love and sacrifice for me.

Your Thoughts…

Day Three

Genesis 1:26

Then God said, "Let us make man in our image, in our likeness, and let them rule over the fish of the sea and the birds of the air, over the livestock, over all the earth, and over all the creatures that move along the ground"

*Hebrew**(read right to left!)*

ויאמר אלוהים: "נעשה אדם בצלמנו בדמותנו למען ימשול בדגה שבים ובעוף שבשמ

ובבהמה ובכל חיות הבר ובכל רומש הארץ".

My Dad said to me once, "you know man wrote that verse because humans are ugly, why would you want that." Dad was missing the true meaning. The image is not physical. (thank you, Lord, because yes, we are kind of ugly as creatures go) The image is spiritual. God's image is spiritual and we are created in HIS image. How we picture God as an old man with a long white beard is stuff of fairy tales. I'm going to bet He is not like that. However, when we die do we retain the same form? I'm going to bet not because we are imperfect in this form. We will not need form. It is our spirit that is our image. We will know each other by that image. These bodies are temporary (again, thank you Lord) Our spirit is eternal.

Prayer**God, your image is not something I can comprehend in this world. The beauty of this world also has flaws. I long to see your image and worship you. I look forward to my image being perfected by and for you.

Your Thoughts…

Day Four

Jonah 4:11b

full verse" but Nineveh has more than a hundred and twenty thousand people who cannot tell their right hand from their left, and many cattle as well. Should I not be concerned about that great city?"

*Hebrew***

והלא עלי לדאוג לעיר הגדולה נינווה, אשר בה חיים יותר ממאה ועשרים אלף איש

אשר אינם יכולים להבחין בין ימינם לשמאלם, וגם בהמות רבות?

God created it all. Every single cell. With that being said, would it not stand to reason that he is concerned and loves it all? Absolutely! I point to this verse because to me it shows God cares about the animals. He created them for our use and we must take care of them. Many people argue that animals do not go to heaven. I believe animals do. God does not explicitly say it here, but it leans that way. If it was not a thing why mention it? Now we all have pets of various species. We love them and call them part of the family. What do we say to them, "oh you are such an angel!" (except my Ellie, she is a mafia hitman) I think they are angels. Simply put, God created angels, they are not dead humans, they are creatures to serve and companionship. Earthly pets serve the same purpose. Yes, our pets and animals do go to heaven and they exist here as angels.

Prayer**I love my pets. Thank you for creating something for me to love as you love your angels. The peaceful existence of animals with man is truly heavenly. I look forward to eternity with all angels, heavenly and earthly.

Your Thoughts…

Day Five

1 Samuel 20:4

Jonathan said to David, "Whatever you want me to do, Ill do for you."

*Hebrew***

"ויאמר יהונתן לדוד: "כל אשר תרצה שאעשה, אעשה לך.

Do you have a best friend? What would you do for your best friend? Jonathon and David were the best of friends. Jonathon loved David. Jonathon would do whatever David desired. Did he say that as loyalty to a friend or future king? If you look back a chapter you will see Jonathon speak well of David to Saul, David's enemy. David loved Jonathon too. I'm just going to assume here that maybe they grew up together, they played together in pastures, they teased each other about girls. They were best friends, brothers. They knew who was on their side. We read about this friendship because as with all scripture, God is teaching us. In this case God is teaching us what true friendship is.

Prayer**My friends are the world to me. I love them and look out for them. Thank you, God, for showing how friends are to care for each other and live life together after your heart.

Your Thoughts…

Day Six

Isaiah 53:4-5

Surely he took up our infirmities and carried our sorrows, yet we considered him stricken by God, smitten by him, and afflicted. But he was pierced for our transgressions, he was crushed for our iniquities; the punishment that brought us peace was upon him, and by his wounds we are healed.

*Hebrew***

אמנם כאבנו נשא, סבלנו נשא, ואנחנו ראינו אותו נעגש מאת אלוהים, מוכה ממגו

ועונה. והוא נוקב על פשעינו, הוא נמחץ על עוונותינו; עונש שלום היה עליו,

ובפצעיו נרפאנו.

A prophecy of the savior to come. Try to read this and not think about Jesus. It is hard to do but try. A man that took all our screw ups onto himself. God smacked. Brutalized. This is the death any human deserves. No one however could endure this torture and torment knowing death was imminent. Now put Jesus there. He is God. God stepped down from royalty to clean up our failures, our pure stupidity. Jesus suffered for us to pay God. This is the ransom. This is pain and yet the most perfect love. Parents, would you not suffer for your child to save them? Imagine that love an infinite amount of times. It is impossible to comprehend, yet God prepared this since the beginning of time. The pain, the anguish, the ultimate love.

Prayer**Your love for me is indescribable. It is a sacrifice. It is a purpose. It is a love that I will never understand on Earth. I pray to you to continue to show me that love until I see you in Heaven.

Your Thoughts…

Day Seven

Jonah 1:3

But Jonah ran away from the Lord and headed for Tarshish. He went down to Joppa, where he found a ship bound for the port. After paying the far, he went aboard and sailed for Tarshish to flee from the Lord.

*Hebrew***

ויברח יונה מפני יהוה וירד את־יופא וימצא אנית הנמה הנמה. ויֹשלם את־הדר ויֹרשים

את־האנית ויֹרשים מפני יהוה

When have you run from your issues? When has an issue so overwhelmed you that you thought your only solution was to avoid it. We have all done it or at least have tried. When did you run from someone that was given orders you did not like? We have all done that too. Jonah was running from God. GOD. It makes me laugh at the notion. God wanted him to do a few things and Jonah put up a fight. Jonah hated Nineveh. He thought the people were trash. Jonah also did not care for the hand he was dealt. He was what we term as a minor prophet. He may have been a prophet of God but he was kicking and screaming the whole time. He tried to flee from God because he did not want to do what was required. Funny though, God got him. He ultimately did what he was told. Running from God was futile. Face God, handle your issues now and do not delay. You will just look back saying, "it could have been over by now." Do it now. Do what you are told to do.

Prayer**God, you are my ruler, lord, and father. I know I ignore you a lot and do not do what I'm told. Help me hear that your command and your sweet whispers are for my own good and I do not have a corner on knowing what is best for me.

Your Thoughts…

Day Eight

Matthew 6:25

Therefore I tell you, Do not worry about your life, what you will eat or drink; or about your body, what you will wear. Is not life more important than food, and the body more important than clothes?

*Greek**Διὰ τοῦτο λέγω ὑμῖν, μὴ μεριμνᾶτε τῇ ψυχῇ ὑμῶν τί φάγητε [ἢ τί πίητε] μηδὲ τῷ σώματι ὑμῶν τί ἐνδύσησθε. οὐχὶ ἡ ψυχὴ πλεῖόν ἐστιν τῆς τροφῆδ καὶ τὸ σῶμα τοῦ ἐνδύματος:*

Worry. What was the last thing you worried about? It kept you from getting a good night's sleep, didn't it? Did worrying help the situation? Of course it did not. When has worrying about money or your family or your health or anything ever helped or solved the problem. Worrying can actually create more problems. Praying and thinking through the issue with guidance is always the answer. Create a plan of attack. First though you must pray. Ask God for that guidance. Open your heart and mind to God's voice. God will help you every time. Be prepared and conquer but never worry. Worrying just wastes time and energy and you get nothing in return. Trust and obey and you will be blessed with a solution and ready to tackle the next issue.

Prayer**I am human. God, you made me, you know I need you. Help me to not worry about things that seem to matter in this life. This life is fleeting. I know I am here to experience this time. Help me open my heart and mind so that your voice is all I need to guide me.

Your Thoughts…

Day Nine

Matthew 7:1-3

Do not judge, or you too will be judged. For in the same way you judge others, you will be judged, and with the measure you use, it will be measured to you. Why do you look at the speck of sawdust in your brother's eye and pay no attention to the plank in your own eye?

*Greek**Μὴ κρίνετε, ἵνα μὴ κριθῆτε· ἐν ᾧ γὰρ κρίματι κρίνετε κριθήσεσθε, καὶ ἐν ᾧ μέτρῳ μετρεῖτε μετρηθήσεται ὑμῖν. τί δὲ βλέπεις τὸ κάρφος τὸ ἐν τῷ ὀφθαλμῷ τοῦ ἀδελφοῦ σου, τὴν δὲ ἐν τῷ σῷ ὀφθαλμῷ δοκὸν οὐ κατανοεῖς;*

These verses are misinterpreted constantly. "I don't support capital punishment because I'm a Christian." "I will not give my opinion because I don't judge." What? These verses are about pettiness. In this day we judge everything on social media. This is petty. People judge the way people live...petty. I even believe that we post on social media to be judged. Likes are a form of judgement and validation. The way people exist is individual between you and God. For anyone to judge you is petty. We are all imperfect. Empathy is needed. Accept people as they are. You do not know their story yet. You are not perfect. You have no authority. Your petty opinion about others is irrelevant. Keep your house in order first.

Prayer**Lord, help me see people as they are. I do not care for their opinion so why would they care about mine. We are all in the same imperfect world at different levels of imperfection. Guide me to be better daily and empathize with others and help them as needed.

Your Thoughts...

Day Ten

The next few days we will be in Philippians. Paul's letter to the Phillipians has some great advice about faith and how to live in this world. Let us begin.

Philippians 2:3

Do nothing out of selfish ambition or vain conceit, but in humility consider others better than yourselves.

*Greek**μηδὲν κατ' ἐριθείαν μηδὲ κατὰ κενοδοξίαν ἀλλὰ τῇ ταπεινοφροσύνῃ ἀλλήλους ἡγούμενοι ὑπερέχοντας ἑαυτῶν,*

Empathy. Our life is not all about us. Unless you live in a cave thousands of miles from another life. Your life is a constant interaction with other people. Humility is the humbling before another person, but mainly before God. Be humble. Be empathetic to others. Be worthy. There is nothing sinful about taking care of yourself but the care you show yourself is to be shown more so to others. Be better always.

Prayer**My life is a gift you have given me, God. Thank you so much for this experience. Guide me to be grateful daily. Help me be there for others as they need me.

Your Thoughts…

Day Eleven

Philippians 4:1

Therefore, my brothers, you whom I love and long for, my joy and crown, that is how you should stand firm in the Lord, dear friends!

*Greek**Ὥστε, ἀδελφοί μου ἀγαπητοί καὶ ἐπιπόθητοι, χαρὰ καὶ στέφανός μου, οὕτως στήκετε ἐν κυρίῳ, ἀγαπητοί.*

Promises of peace. Paul writes to the Philippians to encourage them in their walk. In this chapter he outlines only as Paul can, five steps or more specifically five promises of peace and joy. First and foremost, stand firm in the Lord. Know with your mind, body and soul that God, Jesus, Spirit are one. They are never wrong, always protecting and providing. Go with confidence knowing God.

Prayer**How well do I know you, God? When things are bad, I pray but when things are good, do I pray? Every day I need to see you in your glory and I need to bring this to the fore. Thank you, Jesus, for what you did for me. I am not worthy, but you are beyond pure love and your love for me is hard to comprehend but I am willing to learn.

Your Thoughts…

Day Twelve

Philippians 4:4

Rejoice in the Lord always. I will say it again: Rejoice!

*Greek**Χαίρετε ἐν κυρίῳ πάντοτε· πάλιν ἐρῶ χαίρετε.*

Knowing the Lord and going into life confidently leads to rejoicing. Every day no matter what mood you wake up in, no matter what other people do in the office or on the road, just stop. Stand firm and rejoice. Sounds counterintuitive but try it. Your mood will change almost instantly. Feel the joy from deep inside. That is the Holy Spirit making his presence known thoroughly. (also, forgive that co-worker or driver and move on)

Prayer**God, some days are just in my face. Sometimes I want to lash out to whomever for whatever because I'm grouchy. Guide me to find that joy, YOU, deep inside and know that you are all that matters.

Your thoughts…

Day Thirteen

Philippians 4:6

Do not be anxious about anything, but in everything, by prayer and petition, with thanksgiving, present your request to God.

*Greek**μηδὲν μεριμνᾶτε, ἀλλ' ἐν παντὶ τῇ προσευχῇ καὶ τῇ δεήσει*

μετὰ εὐχαριστίας τὰ αἰτήματα ὑμῶν γνωριζέσθω πρὸς τὸν θεόν.

This point is brought up other times in the New Testament. Stop worrying. STOP IT! All worrying does is waste time and energy. (See Day Eight) Think about what you could be doing instead of all that worrying. Thanking God, perhaps? Better yet, trusting and praising God. Yet we all worry, but stop and think this…Did anything I worried about help the situation. I bet I know your answer. Focus!

Prayer**God, it is in my sin nature to worry but thank you for helping me see that when I worry, I immediately realize that I am trusting you less. For my worries are just second guessing what you did/do/will be doing in my life. Worry is not worth my distrust.

Your Thoughts…

Day Fourteen

Philippians 4:7

And the peace of God, which transcends all understanding, will guard your hearts and your minds in Christ Jesus.

*Greek**καὶ ἡ εἰρήνη τοῦ Θεοῦ ἡ ὑπερέχουςα πάντα νοῦν φαρουρήςει*

τὰς καρδίας ὑμῶν καὶ τὰ νοήματα ὑμῶν ἐν Χριστῷ Ἰησοῦ.

Once you learn to control, or better yet, stop worrying, the peace you will feel from God will be something amazing. Your heart will be on fire and protected. Your mind will focus clearer on Jesus. Worrying clogs the flow. Focus to open. Focus on Jesus. Let the Holy Spirit loose.

Prayer**God, thank you for always everyday helping me see that the world you created is a wonder. I should not worry about that wonder because you are in control. I yearn for the fire in my heart and the clear focus on my mind. Every day I look to you.

Your Thoughts…

Day Fifteen

Philippians 4:9

Whatever you have learned or received or heard from me or seen in me—put it into practice.

*Greek**ἅ καὶ ἐμάθετε καὶ παρελάβετε καὶ ἠκούσατε καὶ εἴδετε ἐν ἐμοί,*

ταῦτα πράσσετε·

Now do it! Stop worrying. Do not waste any more time and energy. Find joy by focusing on God. He has your back. I have a thought that all these issues are little demons from satan to take our focus off God. Satan's main focus is to distract, lie, and make us sacrifice our faith in God. So, his demons are named, worry, loneliness, fear, anxiety, boredom, etc. All these demons can be sent packing when we focus on God and that is scary to satan.

(note…I refuse to capitalize THAT proper name unless the beginning of a sentence.)

Prayer**You got me. Thank you, God.

Your Thoughts…

Day Sixteen

Philippians 4:11

I am not saying this because I am in need, for I have learned to be content whatever the circumstances.

*Greek**οὐχ ὅτι καθ' ὑστέρησιν λέγω, ἐγὼ γὰρ ἔμαθον ἐν οἷς εἰμι αὐτάρκης εἶναι.*

This is a very familiar verse. Learn to be content in all circumstances. Paul was in custody in Rome when he wrote this. His situation was dire, but he managed to be safe in God's hands and be content. I'm sure he was concerned but he did not worry about it. He raised his voice to God and his heart was blessed with contentment. Do not dwell but find the lesson. Feel the presence.

Prayer**Being content in all circumstances is very hard, however, I know you are with me. You are holding my hand in times of trouble and grinning on me in times of joy. That is enough for me to be content in all circumstances with you by me.

Your Thoughts…

Day Seventeen

Philippians 4:13

I can do everything through him who gives me strength.

*Greek**πάντα ἰσχύω ἐν τῷ ἐνδυναμοῦντί με.*

Do you get tired often? Do you want to work forward yet are exhausted mentally and physically? Where do you find the strength to move forward? Paul writes to the Philippians while in jail. He was suffering physically and I am sure suffered mentally. Yet he had the strength or power to do what needed to be done all because of Christ. Christ is power. Christ is strength. Christ is the antithesis of exhaustion. Go forth!

Prayer**God, some days are just so long and tiring. People at work wear me down mentally. Running errands that need to be done wear me down physically. Existing is exhausting. I look to you today and every day for the power and strength to exist every day. Thank you for always being with me.

Your Thoughts…

Day Eighteen

Ephesians 4:2

Be completely humble and gentle; be patient, bearing with one another in love.

*Greek**μετὰ πάσης ταπεινοφροσύνης καὶ πραΰτητος, μετὰ μακροθυμίας, ἀνεχόμενοι ἀλλήλων ἐν ἀγάπῃ,*

This verse is the essence of life as a Christian. Be humble. We read about not being boastful in the Old Testament a few times. Keep your head down and get to work for Christ. Do not announce it, just do it. Be gentle. Who was the gentlest since time began? He is who we must strive to be like. Be patient. Prove to me how things will get done when you are antsy, grouchy, running all around, i.e., impatient. It is a worthless exercise and wastes a lot of energy. Just relax and focus. Use your talents. Activate your mind to think through that which you struggle. Be in love. Not the lust kind of love but love of another, the love of God. Love his creation. Love one another for you love God and all he does. We do not have to like each other but we love and respect each other as part of God's wonderful creation.

Prayer**God, I bow before you in thanksgiving and awe. You made me and everything I know and it is beautiful. Getting tied up in the world is easy to do but knowing I can step out of it and be with you whenever I like is comforting and powerful.

Your Thoughts…

Day Nineteen

1 Thessalonians 5:16-18

Be joyful always; pray continually; give thanks in all circumstances, for this is God's will for you in Christ Jesus.

*Greek**Πάντοτε χαίρετε, ἀδιαλείπτως προσεύχεσθε, ἐν παντὶ εὐχαριστεῖτε· τοῦτο γὰρ θέλημα θεοῦ ἐν Χριστῷ Ἰησοῦ εἰς ὑμᾶς.*

These are our orders. Don't gripe. Always be talking with God. No matter the situation, give thanks. No matter if it seems good or bad to us, God is working that situation to prosper us. So be talking with him to hear about the plans. Stop belly aching. Ok, yes, easier said than done but strive for it all.

Prayer**Every day is a challenge. People are annoying. Situations are unplanned. All I want to do is complain and be grouchy. However, I know what I need to do. Focus on you and let go of this world. The pain here will one day be washed away for your glory. Remind me daily.

Your Thoughts…

Day Twenty

1 Thessalonians 5:19-22

Do not put out the Spirit's fire; do not treat prophecies with contemp. Test everything. Hold on to the good. Avoid every kind of evil.

*Greek**τὸ πνεῦμα μὴ σβέννυτε, προφητείας μὴ ἐξουθενεῖτε, πάντα δὲ δοκιμάζετε τὸ καλὸν κατέχετε, ἀπὸ παντὸς εἴδους πονηροῦ ἀπέχεσθε*

These verses continue the orders given yesterday. Move forward with grace and humility. Stop being negative in your self-talk and towards others. Evil takes many forms and once it roots it is like a weed. It takes a lot of treatment to get rid of it. Do not let the evil take root. It is ok to question, it is how we learn, but focus on what is good.

Prayer**The world is filled with evil. Things that are very appealing to my senses. Please help me distinguish between what is evil and what is yours, God. My focus is on you.

Your thoughts…

Day Twenty-One

1 Timothy 6:16

who alone is immortal and who lies in unapproachable light, whom no one has seen or can see. To him be honor and might forever. Amen

*Greek**ὁ μόνος ἔχων ἀθανασίαν φῶς οἰκῶν ἀπρόσιτον, ὅν εἶδεν οὐδεὶς ἀνθρώπων οὐδὲ ἰδεῖν δύναται· ᾧ τιμὴ καὶ κράτος αἰώνιον, ἀμήν.*

Intense. Paul is telling Timothy about God. These attributes are very intense. Reread that verse. Picture it the best you can. The light shines brighter than our eyes can handle. Be worthy to try.

Prayer**Your light is all the light I want and need.

Your thoughts…

Day Twenty-Two

In the next few days we will delve into the Sermon on the Mount in Matthew 5. What are the Beatitudes? "Blessed are…" the beauty of this teaching. Let us begin…

Matthew 5:3

Blessed are the poor in spirit, for theirs is the kingdom of heaven.

*Greek**Μακάριοι οἱ πτωχοὶ τῷ πνεύματι, ὅτι αὐτῶν ἐστιν ἡ βασιλεία τῶν οὐρανῶν.*

Poor in spirit. Would that not mean their faith is weak or their soul is weak. No exactly. Here the poor are the babies in the faith. Their faith is new and growing and their soul is wanting. They are not faithless. They are quite faithful but very new to it. Strength comes and their future is to serve in the Kingdom. Are you poor yearning to grow?

Prayer**Lord, being new to the faith is exciting and intimidating. Help me find guidance to be able to serve you on earth and Heaven.

Your Thoughts…

Day Twenty-Three

Matthew 5:4

Blessed are those who mourn, for they will be comforted.

Greek**Μακάριοι οἱ πενθοῦντες, ὅτι αὐτοὶ παρακληθήσονται.

As humans we mourn the loss of a lot of things. I mourn the death of family, my cats and even plants. (yes plants. I don't kill them, but their time does come) I have pain in my heart every time I lose a feline critter. They are my family. Yet is this what this verse is talking about? Perhaps. Perhaps not. Jesus could very well be talking about something yet to come. The destruction of all life as we know it. It is prophesied in the last days there will be total destruction. This will destroy the world and we will mourn. However, your faith in Jesus tells you there is something better on the way. Something comforting. Something heavenly. Mourn for the lost that never had faith, mourn for the destruction of everything once created, but be comforted by your new existence. That new existence in the most beautiful and comforting and glorious and loving place. Heaven.

Prayer**Loss is so sad, God. I cry to you when I lose family. I pray you are right next to me holding my hand as I cry. I have learned that everything has its time. I weep today for what is to come in your time. I hope I can help many to find you. I do take comfort in knowing you are all powerful and will take care of this process when the end here comes. It is scary but you are not.

Your Thoughts…

Day Twenty-Four

Matthew 5:5

Blessed are the meek, for they will inherit the earth.

*Greek**Μακάριοι οἱ πραεῖς, ὅτι αὐτοὶ κληρονομήσουσιν τὴν γῆν.*

This beatitude is very common. Blessed are the gentle. The term I always knew was meek is used here. Like with all these it seems contradictory that meek men inherit the earth. However, meek is not weak. The primary definition in Merriam-Webster is 'enduring injury with patience and without resentment'. Enduring and patience, which is ultimately gentle, will inherit the earth. Be gentle in self and with others.

Prayer**Be gentle. Lord, help me be patient and endure this life. My time here is temporary and enduring this life is a challenge. I know being patient is also the key to grace and being gentle as I live. Heaven is my goal but help me live today.

Your Thoughts…

Day Twenty-Five

Matthew 5:6

Blessed are those who hunger and thirst for righteousness, for they will be filled.

*Greek**Μακάριοι οἱ πεινῶντες καὶ δεψῶντες τὴν δικαιοσύνην, ὅτι αὐτοὶ χορταςθήςονται.*

Your time spent studying or reading or talking is very important to growth. Time spent studying the word of God is most important. Do you yearn to hear God speak to you? Do you yearn to understand his words? That yearning to be God's child is a hunger and it leads to righteousness. Strive to be filled everyday. Yearn for the One to fill you up.

Prayer**Lord, I know it is important to commit your words to my heart and soul. Your words are beautiful. My hunger is much and your word is filling. I commit time to be with you and you word.

Your Thoughts…

Day Twenty-Six

Matthew 5:7

Blessed are the merciful, for they will be shown mercy.

*Greek**Μακάριοι οἱ ἐλεήμονες, ὅτι αὐτοὶ ἐλεηθήσονται.*

This one is pretty clear. You show mercy, mercy will be shown to you. This reflects a lot of Biblical teaching in Old and New Testament. Unfortunately, in the world today we see people of all ages feel they 'deserve' this or that and treat others with disdain. I am guilty of this especially when I am driving. There is nothing that is so important for anyone to act the way people do. The old saying, 'what goes around comes around' applies. Expect that. So, be empathetic, be merciful. If not, it will come back on you. Then how will you feel? Show mercy to the most merciless. How? Turn the other cheek. Remember, words are just sound, they can be ignored. Unless you are being physically harmed it is important to show mercy.

Prayer**Lord, it is so hard so many times too be merciful. How can I do this without you? You are with me always I just need that nudge when tempers flair in my heart. Your mercy is amazing to me and I guide my life to be like you with you.

Your Thoughts…

Day Twenty-Seven

Matthew 5:8

Blessed are the pure in heart, for they will see God.

*Greek**Μακάριοι οἱ καθαροὶ τῇ καρδίᾳ, ὅτι αὐτοὶ τὸν θεὸν ὄψονται.*

Pure in heart? Well that rules me out. You too, I am afraid. Does that mean we will not see God? We are broken. We need God. We are not pure, BUT we can be. Our focus needs to be on God in a pure way. Not like, 'well if I do this or that I will get to heaven'. That is not purity that is obligation to what you believer is a ruler or slave diviner. Bargaining does not afford you the key to heaven. But all not be lost, believing in God, loving God, nurturing the relationship is the path to the pure heart. Knowing you have already received eternity with God but still respect and love the relationship is the key to purity and heaven. Put God first.

Prayer**I know it, I know I am a huge sinner. However, I thank you every day for sending Jesus to take my place in death. It is a love I cannot possibly comprehend here on earth. All I can do is praise you, love you, yearn to be with you. I look forward to that day I am in your presence.

Your Thoughts…

Day Twenty-Eight

Matthew 5:9

Blessed are the peacemakers, for they will be called sons of God.

*Greek**Μακάριοι οἱ εἰρηνοποιοί, ὅτι αὐτοὶ υἱοὶ θεοῦ κληθήσονται.*

What is Jesus? The Prince of Peace. God is the King. Throughout life we tangle with others and end up in minor battles. It is human nature to struggle, to try to understand other humans. However, those that strive to bring people together, to bring about peace are a different breed. Personally, I do not enter battles outside of myself, I tend to struggle with in. (even if it is an outside issue) Having an attitude of 'oh well' is what I desire. To bring peace to self and others is a great strength. We all need to focus on peace. Several years ago people had WWJD bracelets. It was a reminder to live bravely and cultivate peace. To stand and be children of God.

Prayer**Peace! It is so hard to put my mind and soul at peace in an increasingly chaotic world. "Do, do, do", is all the world requires of me it seems. I whisper your name and you shine your peace on me. Thank you, Lord, for your peace.

Your Thoughts…

Day Twenty-Nine

Matthew 5:10

Blessed are those who are persecuted because of righteousness, for theirs is the kingdom of heaven.

*Greek**Μακάριοι οἱ δεδιωγμένοι ἕνεκεν δικαιοσύνης, ὅτι αὐτῶν ἐστιν*

ἡ βασιλεία τῶν οὐρανῶν.

Who wants this? I think I can confidently say no one wants to be persecuted for any reason. No one wants pain or anguish. However, we need to remember Jesus said this was not going to be easy, this life. Although following Jesus is the easiest decision to make, it will always be a hard thing to do and at the same time very rewarding. Jesus gave us a command to spread the Gospel and by doing that we will fight people that want to hurt us in many ways. Are you willing to be persecuted for your father? Are you willing to enter evil places for God? Disciples were martyred for Jesus and people today around the world are still being martyred. What will you do or say for Jesus? He is with you through it all. Your reward is Heaven and His presence forever. It is worth the fight. It is worth it all.

Prayer**God, thank you for allowing me to be raised in the best country in the world. In this country we do not have the persecution that occurs in other countries, but we do struggle. Thank you for being an everlasting presence here and by our side as we spread your word.

Your Thoughts…

Day Thirty

Matthew 5:11-12

Blessed are you when people insult you, persecute you and falsely say all kinds of evil against you because of me. Rejoice and be glad, because great is your reward in heaven, for in the same way they persecuted the prophets who were before you.

*Greek**Μακάριοι ἐστε ὅταν ὀνειδίςωςιν ὑμᾶς καὶ διώξωςιν καὶ εἴπωσιν πᾶν πονηρὸν καθ' ὑμῶν [ψευδόμενοι] ἔνεκεν ἐμου. χαίρετε καὶν ἀγαλλιᾶςθε, ὅτι ὁ μισθὸς ὑμῶν πολὺς ἐν τοῖς οὐρανοῖς· οὕτως γὰρ ἐδίωξαν τοὺς προφήτας τοὺς πρὸ ὑμῶν.*

Following yesterday's verse, these verses get alittle more personal. The last verse was the big one. Being persecuted as a whole because of Jesus is going to happen. Jesus said so. Being persecuted personally for Jesus is to mean that everything you do reflects God/Jesus. As we shine love and peace to the uninformed or evil, they will insult you or lie because, and this is the key, they know they are wrong. Be proud, as in honorable, you are insulted for your faith in Jesus. You ARE affecting someone. Then pray for that person or persons that insulted you. You may never know your impact until the day the kingdom comes.

Prayer**It is not easy, God, but I knew the price when I decided you were my love. I will do what I have to do to honor you forever. Thank you for being beside me in this spiritual battle. I will fight for you, lead the way!

Your Thoughts…

Day Thirty-One

Old Testament vs. New Testament

Today's devotional is a slight departure. Today is a history lesson. I encourage you to delve deeper into the history of the Bible and even the Bible languages. The basics are empowering to help defend your faith. Today is about the Old and New Testament…

As Christian the New Testament is our prime read. The question is why do we bother with the Old Testament?

The Old Testament is a set up. It is setting the scene for Jesus. It is the background. The Old Testament is very important for us to understand the 'why' and the 'how' of Jesus. Jesus is talked a3-8bout throughout the Old Testament. Lets go to the beginning. God created. Adam and Eve were allowed by God to fail. This makes no sense on the surface but by them being allowed to fail, it set the stage for a savior. "Why didn't God just restart?" well, first, God makes NO mistake. He created man with a free will to choose Him. He wanted man to come to him by revelation and love. Absolutely God could have made man to love Him obediently and without a choice but that is narcissism. God is love not a despot. God knew man would make mistakes but that is not God making a mistake. It is a freedom for man to think and love and live independently from God, not be a puppet of God. However, man chose poorly with Eve and then Adam. Man is now bound in chains to a sinful nature. Sin entered the world because Adam and Eve used their freewill to think not of God's guidance but selfishly and allowed satan to manipulate them. They chose to disobey and thus set the stage for them being bound and in need of a savior.

Everything in the Old Testament is made clearer because of the New Testament.

The New Testament is the product of Jesus. We stick ourselves in the New Testament because it is very relatable to us. We were raised this way, but the New Testament is only a portion of the whole. Everything in the New Testament relates and references back to the Old Testament.

So when you read that New Testament scripture today, know there is an Old Testament reference. Jesus quotes Old Testament constantly. Footnotes in all the New Testament reference the Old. Spend time looking up those references. I guarantee you will read the Bible wholly and holy complete.

Prayer**Thank you God for inspiring the Bible. Help me commit your words to my heart.

Your Thoughts…

Day Thirty-Two

Genealogy in Matthew (1:1-17)

Today's devotion is a look at Matthew 1:1-17. This is the genealogy of Jesus. Tomorrow we will look at the genealogy in Luke and how they are different.

Big deal, it is an ancestory.com of that time. Yes, it is a big deal. The genealogy of Jesus helps us see the earthly family and prophesy fulfilled. (Old Testament anyone?) Keeping track of ancestry is a very human thing to do. We like to know where we come from. The genealogy websites today are proof. I know, I am Sicilian mainly (explains a lot if you know me) with some Scottish and Irish. Now let us look at this one in Matthew. It starts with Abraham and concludes with Joseph, Jesus' stepdad. Ancestry tracking then was always based on the male's line. Now read through this line again. What are some familiar names? David…royalty. Abraham... the father of nations. It was prophesied that the messiah would be of royal lineage. This is proof.

Prayer**Matthew was writing to the Jewish nation to show the proof of the Messiah and what was prophesized about the Messiah. Thank you for sending Jesus to be that Messiah. He is proof and without a doubt your son, you. Thank you for providing the proof for those that need it.

Your Thoughts…

Day Thirty-Three

Genealogy in Luke (3:23-38)

Today we look at the genealogy list in Luke. This genealogy starts with Jesus and tracks back to Abraham but unlike the genealogy in Matthew, this one goes beyond Abraham to the true father, God.

Names are very much the same as the genealogy at Matthew but the question remains…'why bother?" Actually, this genealogy traces back through Mary. 77 generations which equals completeness and divine perfection. This represents Jesus unrivaled prophesized significant Savior for all.

Take some time and study these genealogy lists. Look for those significant people in both lists. Dig deeper into their lives in the Bible. Now take time to look back at your genealogy. Where is your family from? Again, my great grandfather came from Sicily. My great greats on the other side, came from Scotland and Ireland and ultimately mid Europe. Surely you can see that your family can be traced back ultimately to God. Thank God for your family past, present and future.

Prayer**Luke was a documentarian. I know he wanted the Gentiles to know everything about Jesus. One of the most compelling Gospels. Thank you again, God, for inspiring the Bible to prove Jesus.

Your Thoughts…

Day Thirty-Four

Matthew 6:9-13

This, then, is how you should pray: Our Father in heaven, hallowed be your name, your kingdom come, your will be done, on earth as it is in heaven. Give us today our daily bread.

And forgive us our debts, as we also have forgiven our debtors. And lead us not into temptation, but deliver us from the evil one.

*Greek**Οὕτως οὖν προσεύχεσθε ὑμεις· Πάτερ ἡμῶν ὁ ἐν τοῖς οὐρανοῖς· ἁγιασθήτω τὸ ὄνομά σου· ἐλθέτω ἡ βασιλεία σου· γενηθήτω τὸ θέλημά σου, ὡς ἐν οὐρανῷ καὶ ἐπὶ γῆς· τὸν ἄρτον ἡμῶν τὸν ἐπιούσιον δὸς ἡμῖν σήμερον· καὶ ἄφες ἡμῖν τὰ ὀφειλήματα ἡμῶν, ὡς καὶ ἡμεῖς ἀφήκαμεν τοῖς ὀφειλέταις ἡμῶν· καὶ μὴ εἰσενέγκῃς ἡμᾶς εἰς πειρασμόν, ἀλλὰ ῥῦσαι ἡμᾶς ἀπὸ τοῦ πανηροῦ.*

We all know this. It is the way Jesus taught his disciples to pray. However we know it word for word but do you really KNOW it? These words are fine but that is not exactly what is to be said. This is a guide to praying, it is not to be memorized word for word. Let us break it down.

Verse 9. The Lord name is Holy. Shout it to the world, His name is revered and should always be. Say it like you mean it and in your words however you want to say it.

Verse 10. The Lord's kingdom is glorious and unimaginable. We long for the day this earth is engulfed by Your kingdom and your will.

Verse 11. We know God will provide for our needs, it is ok to ask and you should.

Verse 12. Our sins are great and we repent and ask for forgiveness because we have broken God's laws and more importantly broke his heart.

Verse 13. Guide us like a shepherd guides his sheep to a pasture for lunch. Protect us from the wolves, the evil, that lurk.

This prayer does not have to be word for word but the meaning must be the same.

Prayer**God your name is holy and lovely and powerful, I wait with anticipation for your home to be my home here and in Heaven. I am sorry, please forgive me. Be my leader and protector forevermore.

Your Thoughts…

Day Thirty-Five

Reflection on The Lord's Prayer

Yesterday I broke down the Lord's Pray in Matthew 6. The Sermon on the Mount that is most specific appears in Matthew. Luke does present the Sermon on the Mount but slightly different and different points are emphasized. With that in mind, I encourage you to compare. Today I am just talking about Matthew's Lord's prayer from the sermon.

Yesterday was a total breakdown of the prayer. There are four parts, thus four thing Jesus is saying God wants to hear from us specifically when we talk to Him.

1. First you must honor the one you are talking to. You honor a judge, right. You honor your parents, correct. You honor authority. Honor the most of all those things and more. 'God, your name is above all names…" HONOR.
2. Be thankful. Be thankful spiritually that God loves you. Tell him that. Most of my prayers in this devotional say 'thank you'. I could not do it alone because I am not alone so THANK YOU.
3. Ask forgiveness. Beg humbly. We break God's laws every day. EVERYDAY! He will forgive but we must ask for it. Repent, Do better, fulfill your promise to Him. Your words need to be part of your actions. ASK
4. Ask to be protected. Evil is around us constantly. Evil loves when our minds wonder to anything but God. We need a protector. Ask God to cover us with his protection. He will. ASK

This prayer is what is called a corporate pray because it says a lot of 'we' and 'our', a group prayer. That is church. We come together to corporately pray to God and for his people along these 4 points but individually these points are important. If you are not honoring or thanking or asking God on a personal basis, what are you doing? Strengthening your personal prayer will help strengthen the church's prayer and the church.

Prayer**Oh Holy God, thank you for everything in this world and in the next. Forgive my sin nature and guide me to be better. Protect me from the evil that surrounds me. Your kingdom I long for and your glory is what I ache in my heart to be in your presence.

Your Thoughts…

Day Thirty-Six

John 20:24-31

Now Thomas (also known as Didymus), one of the Twelve, was not with the disciples when Jesus came. So the other disciples told him, "We have seen the Lord!" But he said to them, "Unless I see the nail marks in his hands and put my finger where the nails were, and put my hand into his side, I will not believe." A week later his disciples were in the house again, and Thomas was with them. Though the doors were locked, Jesus came and stood among them and said, "Peace be with you!" Then he said to Thomas, "Put your finger here; see my hands. Reach out your hand and put it into my side. Stop doubting and believe." Thomas said to him, "My Lord and my God!" Then Jesus told him, "Because you have seen me, you have believed; blessed are those who have not seen and yet have believed." Jesus performed many other signs in the presence of his disciples, which are not recorded in this book. But these are written that you may believe that Jesus is the Messiah, the Son of God, and that by believing you may have life in his name.

*Greek**Θωμᾶς δὲ εἷς ἐκ τῶν δώδεκα, ὁ λεγόμενος Δίδυμος, οὐκ ἦν μετ' αὐτῶν ὅτε ἦλθεν Ἰησοῦς. ἔλεγον οὖν αὐτῷ οἱ ἄλλοι μαθηταί, Ἑωράκαμεν τὸν κύριον. ὁ δὲ εἶπεν αὐτοῖς, Ἐὰν μὴ ἴδω ἐν ταῖς χερσὶν αὐτοῦ τὸν τύπον τῶν ἥλων καὶ βάλω τὸν δάκτυλόν μου εἰς τὸν τύπον τῶν ἥλων καὶ βάλω μου τὴν χεῖρα εἰς τὴν πλευρὰν αὐτοῦ, οὐ μὴ πιστεύσω.Καὶ μεθ' ἡμέρας ὀκτὼ πάλιν ἦσαν ἔσω οἱ μαθηταὶ αὐτοῦ καὶ Θωμᾶς μετ' αὐτῶν. ἔρχεται ὁ Ἰησοῦς τῶν θυρῶν κεκλεισμένων, καὶ ἔστη εἰς τὸ μέσον καὶ εἶπεν, Εἰρήνη ὑμῖν.εἶτα λέγει τῷ Θωμᾷ, Φέρε τὸν δάκτυλόν σου ὧδε καὶ ἴδε τὰς χεῖράς μου, καὶ φέρε τὴν χεῖρά σου καὶ βάλε εἰς τὴν πλευράν μου, καὶ μὴ γίνου ἄπιστος ἀλλὰ πιστός. ἀπεκρίθη Θωμᾶς καὶ εἶπεν αὐτῷ, Ὁ κύριός μου καὶ ὁ θεός μου.λέγει αὐτῷ ὁ*

Ἰησοῦς, Ὅτι ἑώρακάς με πεπίστευκας· μακάριοι οἱ μὴ ἰδόντες καὶ πιστεύσαντες.Πολλὰ μὲν οὖν καὶ ἄλλα σημεῖα ἐποίησεν ὁ Ἰησοῦς ἐνώπιον τῶν μαθητῶν [αὐτοῦ], ἃ οὐκ ἔστιν γεγραμμένα ἐν τῷ βιβλίῳ τούτῳ·ταῦτα δὲ γέγραπται ἵνα πιστεύ[σ]ητε ὅτι Ἰησοῦς ἐστιν ὁ Χριστὸς ὁ υἱὸς τοῦ θεοῦ, καὶ ἵνα πιστεύοντες ζωὴν ἔχητε ἐν τῷ ὀνόματι αὐτοῦ.

Although a long passage, the point is clear. Have you ever been called a 'doubting Thomas'? It is a slight, not a compliment. This is from where that comes. Thomas was one of the original twelve. Nothing before these verses alludes to anything unique about him. He was called and he followed. Then, the drama of Jesus last hours. The disciples scattered at first, but they met up again. Jesus appeared to ten of them. Thomas was not among them at this meeting. A week later Thomas was there, Jesus appeared, and Thomas did not believe it was him, without the proof of touch. Do you doubt without proof? Somethings you must have proven but faith is a belief in what is unseen. Thomas did not have that.

God is everywhere. This is his creation but having to see HIM face to face should not be necessary to know he is Lord of all. Let the spirit prove it to you. Let the Spirit help strengthen your faith to believe in what is unseen.

Prayers**Dear God, your glory is alive and well in your creation. In the Earth land, animals and humans. Our faith is weak at times. Let your Holy Spirit settle on us to show us you are you during times we doubt.

Your Thoughts...

Day Thirty-Seven

James 2:22

You see that his faith and his actions were working together, and his faith was made complete by what he did.

*Greek** βλέπεις ὅτι ἡ πίστις συνήργει τοῖς ἔργοις αὐτοῦ καὶ ἐκ τῶν ἔργων ἡ πίστις ἐτελειώθν,*

James is bold. James is in your face. James calls it like he sees it. What does he have to lose? James is Jesus' half-brother and will defend and preach on his behalf. In this verse he is referring to Abraham and Issac. Abraham was told by God to sacrifice Issac. Abraham obeyed but right before the sacrifice an angel stopped him. We do not know how Abraham felt about sacrificing his son however, he remained faithful to God throughout the process. God tested Abraham's faith with an order of action. James simply states Abraham's action and faith were in sync and thus his faith was made stronger. God made Abraham the father of all nation to come because of that faith.

Prayer**Holy God, only you know the beginning and end of my life. Only you know the strength and weaknesses I will face in myself. Test me as you will as I know with all my heart you are with me.

Your Thoughts…

Day Thirty-Eight

1 Timothy 6:10

For the love of money is a root of all kinds of evil. Some people, eager for money, have wandered from the faith and pierced themselves with many griefs.

Greek**ρίζα γὰρ πάντων τῶν κακῶν ἐστιν ἡ φιλαργυρία, ἧς τινες ὀρεγόμενοι ἀπεπλανήθησαν ἀπὸ τῆς πόστεως καὶ ἑαυτοὺς περιέπειραν ὀδύναις πολλαῖς.

I first remember seeing this verse on a TV show. There was a plaque on the wall in the background that said, 'Money is the root of all evil" (100pts if you know what show I speak of…email me if you know) I remember telling my mom this and she corrected me. It is not money itself; it's the love of money. I looked it up. She was right. The love of money is the root of all kinds of evil. I look at it this way, if you love something with a passion then it becomes what you worship, your god. Sure, we say, 'oh I love that house' or 'I love that vacation spot', this is not the passion I speak of. It is when something rules you, dictates your life. Money can do that to people. When you are up nights thinking about how much money you need to do this or that or be this or that. You have a god. Money is just a thing, not a god. Stop treating it like it has power. History shows a lot of people that worshipped money, fell. Worship the one true God.

Prayer**God, money is nothing unless I put value to it. Help guide my heart that you are value and I must look to you not money to solve my problems and guide me towards contentment.

Your Thoughts…

Day Thirty-Nine

Psalm 35:27-28

May those who delight in my vindication shout for joy and gladness; may they always say, "The LORD be exalted, who delights in the well-being of his servant." My tongue will proclaim your righteousness, your praises all day long.

*Hebrew***

ירעו שמחה ושמלה חפצותי; יאמרו תמיד נשם יהוה, חפצה בטוב עבדו. לשוני תגיר

.צדקך, תהלתך כל היום

The title of this psalm is 'The Lord, the Avenger of His People". Take a minute and read the entire psalm. In this psalm David seems to be in conflict. He was a warrior after all. He begs God to vindicate/save him from his enemies. David has always been passionate and dramatic but this psalm he seems to be saying, ENOUGH! I will still praise you, God, just stop this persecution.' The highlighted verses put a stop to the anxiety. 'Supports of me are supports of you. We will always worship you and shout your holiness forever.' Have you gotten to a point where you feel dumped on and wonder what God is doing or where he is? What is your first step? Blame God for the situation, perhaps? Or Praise Him because he is with you? Practice praise in ALL situations.

Prayer**Lord, persecution is part of following you. That is accepted. I know I cannot handle it alone. Please as I am persecuted you will be with me. You may push me to strengthen me but I trust you that you will hold me throughout.

Your Thoughts…

Day Forty

2 Samuel 1:11-12

Then David and all the men with him took hold of their clothes and tore them. They mourned and wept and fasted till evening for Saul and his son Jonathan, and for the army of the LORD and for the nation of Israel, because they had fallen by the sword.

*Hebrew***

ויחזו דוד וכל-האנשים אשר עמו בגדם ויקרעו אתם ויספדו ויבכו ויצמו עד-הערב על-

שאול ועל-יהונתן בנו ועל-ציבא יהוה ועל-עם-יש

David and Saul were bitter enemies. I believe they were mainly because Saul was a narcissist. He could not handle competition yet knew David was to be greater than himself. He hated that. In this chapter David hears of Saul and Jonathan's death. David and Jonathan, Sauls son, were best friends, brothers. They loved each other more than themselves. Now Daivd hears of their death in battle. David is crushed beyond measure. But this pain and mourning was more than the love of his friend. Saul was a leader. David respected that. When Saul's sons were killed in battle, he committed suicide even though he was mortally wounded. Regardless David just lost his friend and his leader. What did this mean for Israel?

Prayer**Dear God, I am here as a representative of you on Earth. People are people and I have my picadilloes. A main one is my dislike for other people. I love some people, I like some people, I would prefer to be away from some people and I hate some people. I know I should not. Help me appreciate all people as your creation. I may not have to love them but help me appreciate them and help me tell them about you love.

Your Thoughts…

Day Forty-One

Leviticus

The Law. The Hebrew Law. The law is what makes people/nation civilized. Without law there is anarchy.

This is the third book of the Torah. The Torah are the books by Moses. The Torah is made up of the first five books of the Old Testament. This book is made up of all the law for the Hebrew's to follow. There are 613 laws and regulations the people had to follow to be closer to God as they wandered in the desert after the exodus from Egypt. The Jewish people today still try to follow all these laws. However it is an impossible task. These laws may have been written to distract the wandering nation as they wandered. Yet they were never meant to be followed, meaning, it is not humanly possible so what was God's plan here? God sent Moses these laws with the point that this is perfection BUT no human can do it so in time 'Ill send perfection'.

I believe Moses knew God had a plan but to pacify the nation of wanderers 613 laws were put in place. 'Follow these laws, nation of Hebrews, and you may just get to the holy land and not get in too much trouble.' Could you imagine if there was no law for that nation? I believe they would still be wandering. The law was thus fulfilled in Jesus.

Prayer**Lord, your law of the Old Testament is so elegant and detailed. Your nation did the best they could but you knew a better way. Thank you so much for the better way. Jesus came to fulfill the laws of your nation, a freedom that is only the beginning.

Your Thoughts…

Day Forty-Two

Nehemiah 1:9

but if you return to me and obey my commands, then even if your exiled people are at the farthest horizon, I will gather them from there and bring them to the place I have chosen as a dwelling for my Name.'

*Hebrew***

ואם-תשובו אלי ותשמׂע את-פקדי, וגמעתם אם-אפק היהי גולתך, ואקבצם משם
ואבאצם אל-המקום אשר-בחרתי לשכם לשכן לישמי.

You are living away from a place you once called home. Your freedoms are limited. Your living arrangements are not the best. You are captive in another land, another nation. The Hebrews were in Babylon, suffering and dying because of their belief. They wanted out. Many assimilated to the Babylon culture, they got out, as it were. Nehemiah was a cup bearer to the king. Nehemiah found favor with the king. So when Nehemiah asked to return to Judah to help with rebuilding the temple, the king granted passage. However, before he returned, Nehemiah had to come to terms with what had happed to the Hebrews and their relationship with God. These verses are part of a quote from Deuteronomy 30, "God will pass you over if you pass him but will gather if you turn back. God is honorable and holy yet YOU have to accept it. It is up to you, lowly human yet created creature, to turn to God.

Prayer**Holy Lord, you are such a loving God. Your desire for your people to be one is echoed throughout what we read. You will bring us together and long for that. Believers long for it as well. We look forward to your kingdom in heaven with your perfect nation.

Your Thoughts…

Day Forty-Three

Genesis 9:5

And for your lifeblood I will surely demand an accounting. I will demand an accounting from every animal. And from each human being, too, I will demand an accounting for the life of another human being.'

*Hebrew***

ועל דם נפשכם אדרוש דין וחשבון. מכל בהמה אדרוש דין וחשבון. וגם מכל אדם

.אדרוש דין וחשבון על נפש אדם אחר

Noah and family just endured the rains, the flooding, the destruction. God now makes a promise to Noah. All the animals of the Earth were under Noah's control and for use for food but with respect and honor must be given to all creatures. Verse Five states that everything that is utilized will be held to account. This really is basic business. Everything money is spent on must be recorded and every dime accounted. Therefore, God told Noah that every drop of blood, human or animal is to be accounted. God also makes a rule here. 'I will judge you and you must not half use the animals or you will have to answer for it. God is giving Noah the world, but Noah must respect and honor that world as it is God's creation.

Prayer**God, the world is your most majestic creation The details in simple things like leaves or more personal things like fingerprints is amazing. Thanks to your command to Noah we have a world full of wonder and beauty. I promise to respect and honor this beautiful world for it is your command.

Your Thoughts…

Day Forty-Four

Nehemiah 4:19-20

Then I said to the nobles, the officials and the rest of the people, "The work is extensive and spread out, and we are widely separated from each other along the wall. Wherever you hear the sound of the trumpet, join us there. Our God will fight for us!"

*Hebrew***

ויאמר לנחרים ולשרים ולשאר העם המלאכה נחיתה ופורשה ואתנחנו פרודים איש

מאלה על־החומה איש מאלה אשר תשמע את־קול־השוצרו שם אלינו

Nehemiah and crew are rebuilding the wall in Jerusalem. Of course there is opposition. Of course people are complaining about the noise or dust or whatever people that want to make no effort, complain about. In these two verses, Nehemiah says we must stick together and finish this work. This is a great metaphor for us as Christians about spreading the Gospel. We must stick together and fight back the dissenters. Evangelical Christians in general are good at this. Missions define us. 'Go forth' is our motto. What about you? Do you talk about Jesus, God, The Bible? Are you attempting to 'go forth'? Do you attend a Bible believing, preaching church? Let us stick together to show and tell the world of God.

Prayer**You Lord are our mission. We go forth and tell everyone about you. Guide us in our mission and put the right words where they are needed. It is not our job to save but it is our job to inform.

Your Thoughts…

Day Forty-Five

The Gospel Writers

Matthew, Mark, Luke, and John. These four books are the crux to all Christianity. They each tell the story of Jesus from birth to resurrection except for John. Matthew, Mark, and Luke are called 'synoptic gospels' since they give a synopsize of Jesus' entire life. John starts where Jesus' ministry starts. Those non-Christians use these differences to say the Bible is inaccurate or contradictory which in fact it is not. HOWEVER and for example, in law enforcement they find that when they are investigating a crime and interview 4 different people, they will get four different stories, but the baseline story is the same. Here we have the same concept. Each writer is telling a story from a different point of view and was written to a different group of readers/listeners.

Matthew was directing his narrative to a Jewish audience

Mark was directing his narrative to a Gentile audience at the time, Romans

Luke was directing his narrative to Gentile Christians

John was directing his narrative to non Jewish believers and unbeliever struggling with Greek philosophies of the time.

Two of the four writers were actual there with Jesus. Matthew was the tax collector that became a disciple and John was the brother of James and the 'one Jesus loved'. Mark is believed to be written by a very close friend of Peter. Luke is written by Luke a physician and companion to Paul. Mark is speculated to have been the first written gospel approximately 60 AD. Matthew 75 AD. Luke 85 AD and John 90 AD. These are just general time frames.

Knowing the audience of each gospel helps to understand the variations of the story. Knowing who was writing the story also helps. Remember though the story is the same through and through. There are no contradictions, there are no missing parts. These are told by individuals from a distinct and different individual perspective.

Now you go tell the story of Jesus. Spread the gospel to all audiences.

Prayer**My life is dedicated to you, Lord based on these four books and all other books in support. Thank you and may my heart grow stronger every day I read your word.

Your Thoughts…

Day Forty-Six

Hebrews 9:28

so Christ was sacrificed once to take away the sins of many; and he will appear a second time, not to bear sin, but to bring salvation to those who are waiting for him.

*Greek**Έτσι ο Χριστός θυσιάστηκε μια φορά για να πάρει μακριά τις αμαρτίες πολλών· και θα φανεί για δεύτερη φορά, όχι για να φέρει αμαρτία, αλλά για να φέρει σωτηρία σε εκείνους που τον περιμένουν.*

This verse is the Bible in summary. God created, man sinned, God knew they would so he sent Jesus, Jesus died for our sins. He will return to bring salvation to all. God came as Jesus. We many not easily comprehend it but our minds are not on the same level as God's. Jesus dies for us. Why? How? We are all born to sin. Yes, we are not born perfect, we may be created perfect but no in this world. God cannot tolerate sin yet loves his creation of us. SO Jesus died to final death for us so we do not have to. A love we, again, cannot comprehend. God in Jesus will return one day and make the world new and beautiful, of which today we cannot comprehend.

Prayer**The wait for Jesus is a longing we all share. We see the sin, we commit the sin, but we believe and love you Almighty Father.

Your Thoughts…

Day Forty-Seven

John 16:33

"I have told you these things, so that in me you may have peace. In this world you will have trouble. But take heart! I have overcome the world."

*Greek**ταῦτα λελάληκα ὑμῖν ἵνα ἐν ἐμοὶ εἰρηνην ἔχητε· ἐν τῷ κόσμῳ*

θλῖψιν ἔχετε· ἀλλὰ θαρσεῖτε, ἐγὼ νενίκηκα τὸν κόσμον.

It is the last Passover feast, Jesus is there to explain to his friends, disciples what is about to happen, what he is and what they are to do. With some, it is not going over very well. Judas has been identified as a betrayer. Peter has been told he is going to fall away in a panic. Yet Jesus explains that the Holy Spirit is coming, He promises. Jesus has told there will not be immediate peace in this world of trouble but He has overcome trouble and all must take heart in Him.

Prayer**Thank you, Jesus for saving me. This world is not easy and quite uncomfortable but you never promised comfort, you promised the Spirit. The Spirit eases tension for me and helps me look forward to your return and your New Jerusalem. I am excited.

Your Thoughts…

Day Forty-Eight

1 Peter 4:8-10

Above all, love each other deeply, because love covers over a multitude of sins. Offer hospitality to one another without grumbling. Each of you should use whatever gift you have received to serve others, as faithful stewards of God's grace in its various forms.

*Greek**πρὸ πάντων τὴν εἰς ἑαυτοὺς ἀγάπην ἐκτενῆ ἔχοντες, ὅτι ἀγάπη καλύπτει πλῆθος ἁμαρτιῶν. φιλόξενοι εἰς ἀλλήλους ἄνευ γογγυσμοῦ, ἕκαστος καθὼς ἔλαβεν χάρισμα εἰς ἑαυτοὺς αὐτὸ διακονοῦντες ὡς καλοὶ οἰκονόμοι ποικίλης χάριτος θεοῦ.*

The New Testament is all about LOVE. Pause here and think about that for a minute, Ill wait…

Peter is writing to groups that have spread far, the Diaspora. He is encouraging them to live and love for God. Yet with a little encouragement to love one another. Look out for everyone's best interest, don't gripe about this process, just do. Help and care of each other as Jesus commanded. As Christians we are to take these words to heart. How often do you wish you did not have to help or chose not to help? All the time. We all grip about it at one time or another. But you know what, helping in different ways, giving financially or giving of time, makes your heart smile, does it not? Oh you know it does. My giving has changed over the years, yours likely has too but know that giving means something. Do not do it if you are going to complain about it. It is not worth it then. Give and know you mean something to others because they mean something to you.

Prayer**Thank you Lord for writing on my heart that I must look out for others lovingly and graciously. People are difficult sometimes but loving them makes me smile. My smile is because you smile.

Your Thoughts…

The next seven days will be of a general nature. I will be talking in general about a few different topics. I encourage you to do your own research and scripture review of these topics.

Day Forty-Nine

Disciples and Apostles

Each gospel talks about the 12 disciples chosen by Jesus. Disciple is just a fancy word for follower and student and apostle is one sent on a mission. We are all disciples but are you and apostle? Many church denominations are not evangelical.

The Disciples in order of call per Luke. Brothers Peter and Andrew, Brothers James and John sons of Zebedee, Philip, Bartholomew, Matthew, Thomas, James, Simon, Judas, and Judas Iscariot.

Peter was a passionate soul. He wore his heart on his sleeve and he would fight for you. He was destined for greatness and became the cornerstone of the church. The Zebedee boys kind of made fools of themselves and a mockery of why Jesus was here. Mark 10:35-45 is the story of the boys asking to be elevated to the right and left of Jesus. They were not quite there on realizing that those elevated had to suffer like Jesus. Matthew is the evil tax collector. Ooooo. Thomas is doubting. He was a disciple, but his faith was based on things seen and physically felt not on things unseen and believed in his heart. Philip, Bartholomew, James, Simon, and Judas are a company of not mentioned much or at all outside the gospels. This is not to say they did not do the work and spread the word, they just did it in a way that did not require to be written down. And of course, Judas Iscariot. Poor Judas, his love of money and power was all kinds of evil.

In Acts 6 we see more apostles emerge. This is not an exhaustive list. Stephen, vs 5, a man full of faith and of the Spirit. Later stoned a martyr. Phillip, the Evangelist. He was a world traveler. Samaria to Ethiopia. No this is not the same Philip as the disciple. Procorus, Nicanor, Timon, Parmenas, and Nicolas round out the seven named.

By the time the apostles in Acts 6 are named the faith has grown exponentially in the region. A world awaited them.

Prayer**Because of this group of men and the many many during and after have a faith and knowledge of you, Lord. My thanks for their sacrifice and love.

Your Thoughts…

Day Fifty

Genesis 2 & 3

Adam and Eve. Eve and the snake. The snake and man. The fall of man.

These two chapters are the beginning of the constant battle that follows between man and frankly everything else.

The creation of man is such a lovely and dramatic completion to all of creation. The world was formed but someone needs to be a steward of it. God created man and women, gangly creatures but at the same time, elegant. Two parts of a whole.

Eve made a choice but remember, Adam was right there, he wasn't out fishing. He chose to listen to Eve because the prospect of being knowledgeable about everything. WOW. Wouldn't that be something. Oh how evil is a snake. Evil will play on your desires like nothing else. Evil is beautiful if we are NOT paying attention. God was angry. He created with rules and rules were broken. Banishment but why?

When I was little I ask my mom, why did God not just reset and create man again? Mom's answer was superb and set alittle mind at ease with an easy answer. "Someone would have done it anyway". At the time that was a perfect answer. Many adults, Christian and non, ask the same question. Although mom's answer was a great answer for a young mind, my thinking is now beyond that. Why did God not reset? Yes, he most definitely could but there would not be given the freedom that Adam and Eve had. The freedom to choose or as we call it today, free will. Free will is the choice we all make between God and not God. That is it. God granted us that freedom. He already knows our mind and heart but we have to come to the conclusion ourselves or there is no freedom.

Within that answer is a deeper meaning. Jesus. All the way at the beginning, God knew he was going to send Jesus. The moment sin reared, Jesus answered. This story is not just a story; this is the beginning salvo. The Old Testament is the battle. The battle against God. The fight that man was trying to prove he did not need a savior. Well we know how that all turned out.

Prayer**God, your creation is mighty. Your love for man is glorious. A mere thank you is not enough to understand that even in the beginning Jesus was there waiting and ready to save us all from evil.

Your Thoughts…

Day Fifty-One

Parables

What are parables? Why are they in the Bible? What makes them so important?

A parable is a short story of moral and spiritual lessons. That simple. They are in the Bible because Jesus was a teacher and sometimes the simplest way to teach is tell a story in a common way. Provoke thought. Jesus was not the only one in the Bible that used parables but his is the most noteworthy. (see 2 Samuel 12)

The importance is as stated. They taught a moral lesson. Everyday life lessons with a twist. The Bible lists 38 parables to Jesus. The most notable ones are in Luke and Matthew.

We know these stories by heart. 1. The Good Samaratian--love and compassion. 2. The prodigal son--forgiveness and redemption. 3. the Sower--everyone receives the message of God's kingdom differently. 4. The lost sheep—each individual is loved by God. 5. The mustard seed—great things come from tiny beginnings.

**Listed in the appendix is all the parables of Jesus and their addresses.

Prayer**Sometimes, God, I need things simplified to understand. The parable technique is perfect. Paint me a picture and teach me a lesson. I am here to learn.

Your Thoughts…

Day Fifty-Two

James

It is widely argued that this letter is by James the half-brother of Jesus. With that, I will hold firm to that claim. I think the content of this letter proves the passion a brother would have for his older brother… and Lord. This letter is very blunt. James does not hold back on anything he writes. Take the time to read this letter from where you are right now in life. It will apply. A quick outline of this letter is as follows…

It was written to various groups scattered and likely poor and possibly oppressed.

First chapter is about how to handle trials and temptations in life. Be humble and continue without anger but joy. Also how to listen, be quick to listen and slow to speak. Don't boost it is unbecoming. "keep a tight rein on your tongue" We encounter a lack of this today. Clearly we haven't changed over time.

Second chapter, James touches on God's favoritism and that IT DOES NOT Exist. The heart is what God cares about not your stuff. Faith and Deeds. Although many Christian believe that you just have to be a good person (deeds) to get to heaven this is NOT what James means. If you have faith, then the deeds, will follow. Faith is the match that lights the deeds of compassion and caring and empathy etc. Its easy to have faith but are you doing what God called you to do with that faith?

Third chapter. Shhhhhh. Were you raised, 'if you cannot say anything nice then don't say it all'? I was. 'Hold your tongue' when you wanted to shout out at someone. James is saying we praise God on Sundays and we are yelling at the minivan driver on Mondays. The yelling is then our identity. Hold fast to the praising and ditch the yelling.

Fourth chapter is very straightforward. Love the world or love God. You cannot have both.

Fifth chapter is also straightforward. I feel a switch as to whom James is talking to at verse 6-7. He is continuing his condemnation in verses 1-6 to those he speaks to in chapter four, the world lovers. At verse 7 his audience is believers. Be good, control yourselves, help each other, be accountable to each other and praise God. A nice way to end.

Prayer**James was a reckoning. I pray for those people to shout from the mountaintops to everyone, believer and non. Thank you, Lord for James' example.

Your Thoughts...

Day Fifty-Three

Major and Minor Prophets

In the Old Testament there are two sections. First are the books of the major prophets and the other are the books of the minor prophets. What makes them major and minor? Were the majors bigger people and more important? Were the minors younger and didn't have clout yet?

Not at all.

The major prophets begin with the book of Isaiah and is followed by Jeremiah, Lamentations, Ezekiel and Daniel. The minors are also considered the twelve. (funny how that number shows up a lot in the Bible) Hosea, Joel, Amos, Obadiah, Jonah, Micah, Nahum, Habakkuk, Zephaniah, Haggai, Zechariah, and Malachi.

What makes them major? The length of the book. The large scope of the context. Thus, then the minor are smaller books and the context is quite narrow in comparison.

A prophet is a someone that speaks for God. Declarations of God. Fantastic. Big deal. Before you poo poo this, know that these prophets declared the coming Messiah, the new Jerusalem and much much more. Jesus fulfilled at least 300 prophesies by these prophets and that is a low estimate. Remember the Old Testament is the foundation for which Jesus will build. (he is a carpenter after all) The reasons why and how and in some cases, when.

Isaiah=judgement, God as King, suffering servant of God. Jeremiah=the weeping prophet is all about judgement, repentance and restoration. Lamentations=judgement, how to respond to that judgement and the character of God. Ezekiel=judgement, God's reign over all, hope in and for future. Daniel=Gods sovereignty, faithfulness to God, apocalypse. The minor Twelve are again more local but the same themes remain, judgement, repentance, faith, restoration.

Take time in the near future and read through the prophets. The themes defined above will jump off the page and may just show you the foundation built with the Old Testament is the reason for your faith today.

Prayer**My God, how the prophets so eloquently speak for you here on Earth. Even today I can see how the prophets are very important to understand you more even in this modern age.

Your Thoughts…

Day Fifty-Four

David

The story of David is found in 1 & 2 Samuel. I could talk for days about David. David first appears in 1Samuel 16. Tending sheep in the field he was called in to ultimately be anointed king by Samuel. He was just a kid, teenager most likely. He was to be king. At this time God had just rejected Saul as king. Saul looked the part. Tall and powerful, expert militarily but he ultimately failed by ignoring God's orders. First however, is not God king? Of course he is but he is a loving God and a teacher. Israel was crying out for an earthly king. They were relentless in this so God gave them what they asked. This became a teachable moment. Here is your earthly king but he will fail. God is the King of Kings. Now back to David, as the relenting continued to have a king, David was going to be next. Saul failed as king. David also fails in many many ways. God loved David but God knew David was weak. David was a man after all, but a man after God's heart.

Take time to read about David in 1 & 2 Samuel. Watch how his friendship with Jonathon is how every friendship should be. Watch how even though Jonathon loved David, his father Saul hated David and tried to kill him. Watch how David matures into an honorable military might yet fails short is so many other ways. It's a soap opera.

David is special and his descendants link right to Jesus via Mary and Joseph. (Matthew and Luke ancestry)

Prayer**God, you loved David and he could be categorized as a screw up. You still loved him. Knowing you loved him in spite of his horrible deeds opens my eyes that you love me too. Thank you, Lord and I love you.

Your Thoughts…

Day Fifty-Five

Exodus 20 vs Deuteronomy 5

1. TV, radio, Social media…not gods so they should go AFTER me not besides or before me.
2. No idols.
3. Do not use my name for stupid sayings, swearing, or 'in the name of' unless I say so
4. Sunday Sunday Sunday!
5. Mom and Dad are supreme just below me
6. Do not murder. Self explanatory.
7. Do not commit adultery. Do I need to go over this one with you all again?
8. Do not steal. You take, I smite
9. Stop lying. Stop it! I know you all do it, STOP IT
10. Keeping up with the Jones is not worth my wrath.

Ten simple but powerful commandments. We see them twice in list form in the Old Testament. However, have you noticed that in the Old Testament they are broken constantly. How about that New Testament…yes, broken. How about your life? Mine, yes. If you read them over and over you see that these commandments are the essence of humanity. Love God, Honor him, Love family and stop wishing or doing bad on others. We fight these commandments every day. Time to stop fighting and now do. Follow them! Jesus did not come to wipe away these commandments, he came to fulfill and strengthen them.

Prayers**Guidance. God your guidance is glorious. As you are with me always, sometimes I need you to yell at me to knock the nonsense off. I know your commands I just need to adhere.

Your Thoughts…

Day Fifty-Six

Romans11:17-21

If some of the branches have been broken off, and you, though a wild olive shoot, have been grafted in among the others and now share in the nourishing sap from the olive root, do not consider yourself to be superior to those other branches. If you do, consider this: You do not support the root, but the root supports you. You will say then, "Branches were broken off so that I could be grafted in." Granted. But they were broken off because of unbelief, and you stand by faith. Do not be arrogant, but tremble. For if God did not spare the natural branches, he will not spare you either.

*Greek**Εἰ δέ τινες τῶν κλάδων ἐξεκλάσθησαν, σὺ δὲ ἀγριέλαιος ὢν ἐνεκεντρίσθης ἐν αὐτοῖςκαὶ συγκοινωνὸς τῆς ῥίζης τῆς πιότη τος τῆς ἐλαίας ἐγένου,[18] μὴ κατακαυχῶ τῶν κλάδων· εἰ δὲ κατακ αυχᾶσαι, οὐ σὺ τὴν ῥίζαν βαστάζεις ἀλλὰ ἡ ῥίζα σέ.[19] ἐρεῖς οὖν, Ἐξεκλάσθησαν κλάδοι ἵνα ἐγὼ ἐγκεντρισθῶ.[20] καλῶς· τῇ ἀπιστίᾳ ἐξεκλάσθησαν, σὺ δὲ τῇ πίστει ἕστηκας. μὴ ὑψηλὰ φρόνει, ἀλλὰ φοβοῦ·[21] εἰ γὰρ ὁ θεὸς τῶν κατὰ φύσιν κλάδων οὐκ ἐφείσατο, [μή πωσ] οὐδὲ σοῦ φείσεται.*

I really wanted to just grab one verse for today, but one verse really is not enough in this example. A tree grows; branches are broken off but others are grafted on. We are all graphs. We are adopted into God's family. We all share in the love of Jesus. We are not to be arrogant about it but be grateful and get to work. We do not support the roots, we grow and learn and help get more grafts. Jesus supports us and our only job is to believe. Obeying and helping others know the word is all part of believing. This is a great passage for the mission we must pursue and an explanation of the life of believers and unbelievers and the last verse is the hard truth. You deny, so will God.

Prayer**Dear God. How you love us. You say it here; you nurture us and help us grow and we are to believe and follow. Strengthen me more daily so I can grow and let others know there is a place for them on the tree.

Your Thoughts…

Day Fifty-Seven

Genesis 45:5

And now, do not be distressed and do not be angry with yourselves for selling me here, because it was to save lives that God sent me ahead of you.

*Hebrew***

ועתה אל-תגעו ואל-תעלו בעל-פניכם, כי-להושיע נפשים שלחני אלהים לפניכם

Joseph was sold by his brothers to traders. Joseph's brothers didn't like him and sold him to be a slave. The brothers then lied to their father, who loved Joseph, tell him Joseph was killed. How deceitful just because you were jealous or angry or whatever negative emotion. Read the story of Joseph then come back to this verse. Joseph was forgiving. Joseph said, yeah you guys did bad to me but God used me to save lives. God controlled this story, boys. God used you to help me to save you and many others. Joseph was right where he needed to be. Have you felt God hasn't used you for anything? Have you looked back on anything significate in your life and said, 'oh hey, God did use me or my situation then" Im going to be you did and He did. Remember God isn't going use us to let bad things happen. Even if bad things happen, God will use you for good. Joseph is the best example. Trust is key at this point. God is teacher and friend. God is going to teach you something but will also be there to comfort you. Focus on Gods abilities not your own in strange situations.

Prayer**Thank you God for being by my side.

Your Thoughts…

Day Fifty-Eight

Roman Road-3:23*5:8*6:23*8:1*10:9

3:23 for all have sinned and fall short of the glory of God,

5:8 But God demonstrates his own love for us in this: While we were still sinners, Christ died for us.

6:23 For the wages of sin is death, but the gift of God is eternal life in Christ Jesus our Lord.

8:1 Therefore, there is now no condemnation for those who are in Christ Jesus,

10:9 If you declare with your mouth, "Jesus is Lord," and believe in your heart that God raised him from the dead, you will be saved.

*Greek**πάντες γὰρ ημαρτον καὶ ὑστεροῦνται τῆς δόξνς τοῦ θεοῦ*

συνίστησιν δὲ τὴν ἑαυτοῦ ἀγάπην εἰς ἡμᾶς ὁ θεός, ὅτι ἔτι ἁμαρτωλῶν ὄντων ἡμῶν Χριστὸς ὑπὲρ ἡμῶν ἀπέθανεν.

τὰ γὰρ ὀψώβυα τῆς ἀναρτίας τγάβατισμ τὸ δὲ χάρισμα τοῦ θεοῦ ζωὴ αἰώνιος ἐν Χριστῷ Ἰησοῦ τῷ κυρίῳ ἡμῶν.

Οὐδὲν ἄρα νῦν κατάκριμα τοῖς ἐν Χριστῷ Ἰησοῦ.

ὅτι ἐάν ὁμολογήσῃς ἐν τῷ στόματί σου κύριον Ἰησοῦν καὶ πιστεύσῃς ἐν τῇ καρδίᾳ σου ὅτι ὁ θεὸς αὐτὸν ἤγειρεν ἐκ νεκρῶν, σωθήσῃ·

Ah the Roman road. Paul writes Romans for he longed to be with them. These five verses are the way to understand what God sent Jesus to do for us and why. These five verses are used in evangelism for that purpose. You can believe in God and that there was a Jesus but these five verses tell you exactly why Jesus was sent and what our simple response must be.

Prayer**Yes Jesus is Lord. My sin is gross. I deserve death. How can I thank you God for Jesus. I will try to live my best life. I fall short daily. Help me focus. Thank you God for Jesus.

Your thoughts…

Day Fifty-Nine

Exodus 32:1

When the people saw that Moses was so long in coming down from the mountain, they gathered around Aaron and said, "Come, make us gods who will go before us. As for this fellow Moses who brought us up out of Egypt, we don't know what has happened to him."

*Hebrew***

וירא העם כי משה התהר ברידה מהר, ויקהלו אל אהרן ויאמרו לך עשה לנו אלהים

וילך לפנינו. ומשה את הזה אשר הולכנו ממצרים, לא

I never understood why the Hebrews were so dang impatient. Just relax people. Slow your roll as the kids say. This whole story line is an amazing test of faith. Moses, trusting and obeying and delivering, with mistakes along the way. Aaron, trusting and obeying Moses, also with mistakes. The people, just trusting the process. The people easily acquired a herd mentality. I am speculating but I will bet one or two people go antsy because they have been wandering and wanted what was promised them. They tell two friends and they tell two friends and on and on. Now everyone is impatient. As you read this story you know God was not happy, Moses wasn't happy…everyone was not happy. How about alittle patience and maybe we all can be happy. The hurrier you go the more behind you get. The promises were just out of arms reach but their impatience made them that much further. Today we hear about the fast food world we live in, Amazon delivery overnight (Amazon is going to tell me to knock it off soon) but I believe that is just a human mentality. They see it and they want it. Hebrews did not have UberEats but they could not wait. How about you slow your roll too.

Prayer**God, why are we so impatient in everything in life? People from the beginning to now have proven to be rather impatient. Please start with me and show me daily that impatience is not getting me anyway fast but rather super slowly. Thank you for YOUR patience with us.

Your Thoughts…

Day Sixty

Ephesians1:4-6

For he chose us in him before the creation of the world to be holy and blameless in his sight. In love he predestined us for adoption to sonship through Jesus Christ, in accordance with his pleasure and will—to the praise of his glorious grace, which he has freely given us in the One he loves

*Greek**καθὼς ἐξελέξατο ἡμᾶς ἐν αὐτῷ πρὸ καταβολῆς κόσμου εἶναι ἡμᾶς ἁγίους καὶ ἀμώμους κατενώπιον αὐτοῦ ἐν ἀγάπῃ προορίσας ἡμᾶς εἰς υἱοθεσίαν διὰ ’Ιησοῦ Χριστοῦ εἰς αὐτόν, κατὰ τὴν εὐδοκίαν τοῦ θελήματος αὐτοῦ, εἰς ἔπαινον δόξης τῆς χάριτος αὐτοῦ ἧς εχαρίτωσεν ἡμᾶς ἐν τῷ ἠγαπημένῳ.*

Did you know, GOD chose you? You are here on this earth because you were created out of love. Yes it is true. God created us and we are made in his spiritual image to be stewards on earth. We are not God. We are his servants. He gave us a very important job. Be fruitful…take care what is given and multiply…create more. We failed (and continue to fail). He sent Jesus to save us from ourselves. He loved us that much. He never gives up on us. He is LOVE. It is predestined. He knew, before human time began, each and every one of us. That is love. He gave us the will to love him back or not. That is our free will. He emphasized it all with Jesus. His Grace is beyond comprehension but his grace keeps us in him.

Prayer**I thank you every day God for the wonders of my life, the world, the grace you have bestowed on all of humanity. Jesus is my lord and my savior from the punishment you would require. Thank you for my lifesaver, my soul saver.

Your Thoughts…

Day Sixty-One

Psalm 40:16

But may all who seek you rejoice and be glad in you; may those who love your salvation always say, "The Lord be exalted!"

*Hebrew** "יִשְׂמְחוּ ... בְּךָ כָּל מְבַקְשֶׁיךָ; יֹאמְרוּ תָמִיד אֹהֲבֵי יְשׁוּעָתֶךָ: "יִשְׂלַם יְהוָה!"*

David knew God. David was the one after God's own heart. David loved God. David praised God in song. This verse seems to say more with less. (I like David already) Throughout this chapter, all David is doing is praising God for protecting and listening and teaching. The last thing he says is for the hope of others to rejoice in God. David was flawed. David did a lot of commandment breaking, more than most of us. Yet God so loved him and he loved God. He knew that God was just and merciful. He knew a savior was needed. Everything is not always perfect for all of us but knowing God will be lessen the blow is something to rejoice. David was king and he let it go to his head but God humbled him and he learned. What a fantastic teacher and father and friend God it.

Prayer**I humbly pray to you, God in thanksgiving and love. My life and love for you is minor compared to your love for me. I long for the day that I am in your presence to feel that love fully. Be my guide as always to tell the people I meet about you.

Your Thoughts…

Day Sixty-Two

1 Peter 3:15-16a

But in your hearts revere Christ as Lord. Always be prepared to give an answer to everyone who asks you to give the reason for the hope that you have. But do this with gentleness and respect,

*Greek**κύριον δὲ τὸν Χριστὸν ἁγιάσατε ἐν ταῖς καρδίαις ὑμῶν ἕτοιμοι*

ἀεὶ πρὸς ἀπολογίαν παντὶ τῷ αἰτοῦντι ὑμᾶς λόγον περὶ τῆς ἐν ὑμῖν

ἐλπίδος, ἀλλὰ μετὰ πραΰτητος καὶ φόβου

Peter never minces words. Know it and do it. He was straightforward in this verse. Always be prepared to explain it because your joy shows. People are attracted to joyful people. Now you have time to tell them why you are joyful. You do not need a pulpit, you do not need a microphone, you need the Holy Spirit to speak to you. It is not easy to share your testimony or the gospel but do it respectfully. You are not converting anyone, your job is just to tell the story. God will convert them. I had an opportunity years ago to share the gospel in downtown Chicago. There was a Muslim family that wanted to hear and they were so taken by what we said they chose to believe, however, there were issues they had to face that prevented them from going all in. I hope they all did come to Christ, I hope they are telling their story in Jesus. **Note** the church I was witnessing with was tasked with follow up. I was gone before I found out how this family was brought into the fold.

Prayer**Being gentle and respectful is key. I know Lord you are the converter but use me however you need so that you, through me, can touch those that need you most.

Your Thoughts…

Day Sixty-Three

Mark 13:33

Be on guard! Be alert ! You do not know when that time will come.

*Greek**Βλέπετε, ἀγρυπνεῖτε· οὐκ οἴδατε γὰρ πότε ὁ καιρός ἐστιν.*

It is going to happen. Today. Tomorrow. 5 years from now. Yes, it is going to happen. Are you ready? Is your heart ready to meet Jesus face to face? You can read this in two different ways. Your personal death, you do not know the time. Or the return of Christ, again, anytime. So shouldn't you be prepared? Be prepared by learning and knowing who Jesus is/was/will always be. Talk to other believers, study the Bible, share with everyone you see, respectfully. I like the little Jesus' that people hand out but it is not enough. If you say thanks but do not know what it is then all you have is a toy. Take the time and prepare your heart, mind and soul for eternity.

Prayer**Everyday could be the day I see you face to face. I try to prepare my soul daily and here I am today preparing. Give me the power to be your representative here on Earth and the preparation to be with you in Heaven.

Your Thoughts…

Day Sixty-Four

11th and 12th Commandments

John 13:34**A new command I give you: Love one another. As I have loved you, so you must love one another. John 13:34

> *Greek**Εντολή νέα σας δίνω: Να αγαπάτε ο ένας τον άλλον. Καθώς σας αγάπησα, έτσι πρέπει και εσείς να αγαπάτε ο ένας τον άλλον.*

Matthew 28:19-20a**Go and make disciples of all nations, baptizing them in the name of the Father and of the Son and of the Holy Spirit and teaching them to obey everything I have commanded you.

> **Greek**πορευθέντες οὖν μαθητεύσατε πάντα τὰ ἔθνη, βαπτίζοντες αὐτοὺς εἰς τὸ ὄνομα τοῦ πατρὸς καὶ τοῦ υἱοῦ καὶ τοῦ ἁγίου πνεύματος, διδάσκοντες αὐτοὺς τηρεῖν πάντα ὅσα ἐνετειλάμην ὑμῖν·**

We know the 10 Commandments. Moses was given these for the Hebrews and before he could show them, they broke most of them. God set the parameters of his justice and his grace too. The Hebrews fell way short. We fall way short too. Falling short is the purpose for Jesus. Adam and Eve set that in motion so one day, the sinful people would need a savior. Jesus came. Although Jesus did fulfill the law and not abolish it he granted us two more commandments to adhere to. The common attribute two both these commands, love. Love each other you know and love all peoples because you are going into it to share Jesus. Love.

Prayer**The Ten Commandments is not just a great movie with Charleton Heston but it is the reason for your people. We all need a baseline and these commandments are it. Jesus showed us more and because you are love, Lord, we have two more commandments to follow. Love. Thank you for your love and tagalong as I love others in your name.

Your Thoughts…

Day Sixty-Five

Hababbuk 3:17-18

Though the fig tree does not bud and there are no grapes on the vines, though the olive crop fails and the fields produce no food, though there are no sheep in the pen and no cattle in the stalls, yet I will rejoice in the LORD, I will be joyful in God my Savior.

*Hebrew***

אם לא-נבל תאנה ולא-יהי ענבים בגפנים, אם-כל יבול הזיתים ולא-יעשיו שדה, אם-

.אין-צאן בדר ולא-בקר בדורים, אשר אשמח בה', אשר אשר גלוג באלהים מושיעי

How can everything be barren and still rejoice in the Lord? How do people do it? It is called faith. Belief in the wonders of God. Belief in the mercy of God. Belief in what God provides. Belief. All this may not be physical things on this Earth. We need to accept and know that God intends good for us not evil. Although evil may happen, it will be worked for good. Look at Joseph in Genesis. He ended up being a savior to his family after his brothers did evil. God allows evil but does not allow it to win. Have faith in the Jesus for he is the savior of this world. Be joyful he loved you so much to save you from the wrath we deserve. Rejoice today is so you can rejoice by his side in heaven.

Prayer**God, it is just a hard concept to grasp sometimes when bad things happen to me. Maybe a lesson is to be learned or maybe it is to teach someone else a lesson. Help me accept that your grace is so important that even when evil happens, you got my back.

Your Thoughts…

Day Sixty-Six

Matthew 2:13

an angel of the Lord appeared to Joseph in a dream. "Get up," he said, "take the child and his mother and escape to Egypt. Stay there until I tell you, for Herod is going to search for the child to kill him."

*Greek** Ἀναχωρησάντων δὲ αὐτῶν ἰδοὺ ἄγγελος κυρίου φαίνεται κατ' ὄναρ τῷ Ἰωσὴφ λέγων, Ἐγερθεὶς παράλαβε τὸ παιδίον καὶ τὴν μητέρα αὐτοῦ καὶ φεῦγε εἰς Αἴγυπτον, καὶ ἴσθι ἐκεῖ ἕως ἂν εἴπω σοι· μέλλει γὰρ Ἡρῴδης ζητεῖν τὸ παιδίον τοῦ ἀπολέσαι αὐτό.*

Why Egypt? Why now? We know the answer to 'why now'. Herod was mad there was someone greater than himself. The Magi told him so. He was so narcissistic that he was not going to let that continue. He was a god, in his own mind. He aimed to kill all the baby boys under two years old. What a crazed narcissist. Yet Egypt. If you remember back in Genesis, Joseph ended up in Egypt and prospered even when his brothers were being evil. Egypt was a rich country. Joseph was honored there. Ultimately, the world went to Egypt because of a worldwide famine. The Hebrews made their home in Egypt then they became slaves to the Egyptians. The rest of that story is in Genesis. Please read and review. But Joseph and Mary are told to flee to Egypt. Again, Egypt is still a rich land and safe. Political borders prevent Herod from going there. Im sure more than just Jesus' family fled to Egypt. Jesus' family was there for years. It is not stated explicitly in the scripture, but he was a tot and then I suspect he was about eleven or twelve upon return. He was twelve or thirteen when he was left behind in Jerusalem at the temple, so ten to twelve years in Egypt. We have two times God had his people go to Egypt.

Could God not keep them safe in Israel? Of course he could but like with anything God does, he is teaching a lesson. What is the lesson? In Joseph's case it was good can come from evil. In Jesus' case? Good will come from evil. Although two different events, they are similar and it is just the way God was teaching. Big shows, like the wilderness, are not necessarily needed but significant meaning is what is important.

Prayer**God you are amazing. Your people of new are not that different than those of old. People are people and we need to be taught who you are by you. Keep teaching me.

Your Thoughts…

Day Sixty-Seven

Hosea 6:3

Let us acknowledge the LORD; let us press on to acknowledge him. As surely as the sun rises, he will appear; he will come to us like the winter rains, like the spring rains that water the earth."

*Hebrew***

נהירה את-ה'; נדרחנה להכרו; כזרח השמש, כן יורא; כגשמי חרף יבא אלינו, כגשמי

אביב הרשים את-הארץ.

I think this verse is self-explanatory. No description needed. A few things to add. Acknowledge and accept the Lord. Love the Lord. Honor the Lord. He is the savior of this world and those that come to him and call him savior will have eternity in paradise.

Prayer**Accepting you Lord is the easiest thing to do. Living life as one of your children can be difficult but I know you are with me and guide me daily. Eternity with you is in my future and I look forward to that day I step out of this world into Heaven.

Your Thoughts…

Day Sixty-Eight

Hebrews 11:1

Now faith is confidence in what we hope for and assurance about what we do not see.

*Greek**Ἔστιν δὲ πίστις ἐλπιζομένων ὑπόστασις, πραγμάτων ἔλεγχος*

οὐ βλεπομένων.

Faith vs. Hope vs. Wishing. Faith is exactly what this verse says, confidence in our hope and assurance in the unseen. Hope is not wishing. This verse does not say, confidence in what we wish for…no. Wishing is a human term. "oh I wish I could do this" "oh I wish I was thinner" "oh I wish they liked me" This is all just wasteful ponderings. Hope is sometimes viewed as wishing but actual hope is knowledge and future truth. I hope in Jesus. I know him and the future truth of his return. I hope in Heaven. I know there is a Heaven and in the future truth of my eternity there. Faith is the leader of hope. Without faith there is no hope. I have faith Jesus is real so I put my hope in him. I have faith in the words of the Bible that there is a Heaven so I put my hope in the eternity I will spend there. Do not just wish, have faith and hope.

Prayer**My faith grows every day in the hope of Jesus. To know you is to have my hope grow and my hope only perpetuates my faith to grow stronger.

Your Thoughts…

Day Sixty-Nine

Mark 16:19-20 and Luke 24:50-53 and Acts 1:9-11

Mark-- After the Lord Jesus had spoken to them, he was taken up into heaven and he sat at the right hand of God. Then the disciples went out and preached everywhere, and the Lord worked with them and confirmed his word by the signs that accompanied it.

Luke--When he had led them out to the vicinity of Bethany, he lifted up his hands and blessed them. While he was blessing them, he left them and was taken up into heaven. Then they worshiped him and returned to Jerusalem with great joy. And they stayed continually at the temple, praising God.

Acts-- After he said this, he was taken up before their very eyes, and a cloud hid him from their sight. They were looking intently up into the sky as he was going, when suddenly two men dressed in white stood beside them. "Men of Galilee," they said, "why do you stand here looking into the sky? This same Jesus, who has been taken from you into heaven, will come back in the same way you have seen him go into heaven."

*Greek** Mark-- Ὁ μὲν οὖν κύριος Ἰησοῦς μετὰ τὸ λαλῆσαι αὐτοῖς ἀνελήμφθη εἰς τὸν οὐρανὸν καὶ ἐκάθισεν ἐκ δεξιῶν τοῦ θεοῦ. 20 ἐκεῖνοι δὲ ἐξελθόντες ἐκήρυξαν πανταχοῦ, τοῦ κυρίου συνεργοῦντος καὶ τὸν λόγον βεβαιοῦντος διὰ τῶν ἐπακολουθούντων σημείων.*

Luke-- Ἐξήγαγεν δὲ αὐτοὺς [ἔξω] ἕως πρὸς Βηθανίαν, καὶ ἐπάρας τὰς χεῖρας αὐτοῦ εὐλόγησεν αὐτούς. καὶ ἐγένετο ἐν τῷ εὐλογεῖν αὐτὸν αὐτοὺς διέστη ἀπ’ αὐτῶν καὶ ἀνεφέρετο εἰς τὸν οὐρανόν. καὶ αὐτοὶ προσκυνήσαντες αὐτὸν ὑπέστρεψαν εἰς Ἰερουσαλὴμ μετὰ χαρᾶς μεγάλης, καὶ ἦσαν διὰ παντὸς ἐν τῷ ἱερῷ εὐλογοῦντες τὸν θεόν.

Acts-- καὶ ταῦτα εἰπὼν βλεπόντων αὐτῶν ἐπήρθη, καὶ νεφέλη ὑπέλαβεν αὐτὸν ἀπὸ τῶν ὀφθαλμῶν αὐτῶν. καὶ ὡς ἀτενίζοντες ἦσαν εἰς τὸν οὐρανὸν πορευομένου αὐτοῦ, καὶ ἰδοὺ ἄνδρες δύο παρειστήκεισαν αὐτοῖς ἐν ἐσθήσεσι λευκαῖς, οἳ καὶ εἶπαν, Ἄνδρες Γαλιλαῖοι, τί ἑστήκατε [ἐμ]βλέποντες εἰς τὸν οὐρανόν· οὗτος ὁ Ἰησοῦς ὁ ἀναλημφθεὶς ἀφ' ὑμῶν εἰς τὸν οὐρανὸν οὕτως ἐλεύσεται ὃν τρόπον ἐθεάσασθε αὐτὸν πορευόμενον εἰς τὸν οὐρανόν.

These three passages describe Jesus' ascension to Heaven. Remember Mark is writing to a Gentile audience. He is brief in his description. Yet for Mark, I think verse 12 is more important; their orders. Our orders. As we know, Luke wrote Acts too. Why did he describe the ascension twice? The Gospel of Luke is about Jesus and Acts is about the apostles. There is a slight overlap but taken separately, and you can, it ends the narrative and then begins the narrative. Jesus ascended to Heaven in front of their eyes. They saw it, just as they saw him after the crucifixion. His death, resurrection and ascension are something we can all know happened and thus believe in Jesus' holiness and God's sovereignty.

Prayer**Proof will always convince someone and to the disciples you gave them proof even when some really did not need it. Jesus is God. You came here to dwell among us to show we can live another way with your help and to know that Heaven is the goal. Thank you, God.

Your Thoughts…

Day Seventy

Matthew 27:24

When Pilate saw that he was getting nowhere, but that instead an uproar was starting, he took water and washed his hands in front of the crowd. "I am innocent of this man's blood," he said. "It is your responsibility!"

*Greek**ἰδὼν δὲ ὁ Πιλᾶτος ὅτι οὐδὲν ὠφελεῖ ἀλλὰ μᾶλλον θόρυβος γίνεται, λαβὼν ὕδωρ ἀπενίψατο τὰς χεῖρας ἀπέναντι τοῦ ὄχλου λέγων, Ἀθῷος εἰμι ἀπὸ τοῦ αἵματος τούτου· ὑμεῖς ὄψεσθε.*

Think about this. On one hand, Pilate was a Roman, could not really care much less about the land he was in only that it was Roman controlled. He did not really want to deal with whatever the Jews were handing him. It was their issue. On the second hand, he was the governor and this was his job. He chose the former. Wash his hands of these people's issue with this man. With that, it sealed Pilate in history as a coward. He chose not to deal with this. Was it because he despised being in Israel? Was it because he was just a figure head in the politics Roman and was just a seat filler masquerading as a governor? You decide. History does not mention Pilate after Israel much if at all. By him not settling the matter did two things, 1. Showed the future what kind of man Pilate was and for that matter the Roman Empire and 2. Allowed the crucifixion and resurrection to occur. Do you ever wonder what would have happened if Pilate told the Jews to hush it and let Jesus go? Hmmm.

Prayer**God, I have to live by the rules of the those that rule on Earth. What is Caesars give to Caesar. Yet I live by your eternal rule. It is like a stepping stone. I try to live peacefully and obediently on Earth to prepare for the wonderful rules of Heaven.

Your Thoughts…

Day Seventy-One

Galatians 3:26

So in Christ Jesus you are all children of God through faith,

*Greek**Πάντες γὰρ υἱοὶ θεοῦ ἐστε διὰ τῆς πίστεως ἐν Χριστῷ Ἰησοῦ·*

This verse harkens back to a verse a few days ago. Believers in Jesus are all adopted children of God. He created us so why are we not just children of God? Well we are but to be adopted children means that 1. We accept a family and 2. God accepted our acceptance. Yes we are children birthright, all humans are but unless you confess Jesus as Savior and God is the father we are not part of that family. Simply put, we may be children of our parents but we are truly children when we do not love and honor them. Biology does not necessarily dictate family. Belief and honor and love is family.

Prayer**Dear God, thank you for loving me from before I was born. You know my life, you know my future. My heart belongs to you, Abba. Thank you for adopting my heart and soul into your family upon my confession.

Your Thoughts…

Day Seventy-Two

Hebrew 3:3

Jesus has been found worthy of greater honor than Moses, just as the builder of a house has greater honor than the house itself.

*Greek**πλείονς γὰρ οὗτος δόξης παρὰ Μωϋσῆν ἠξίωται, καθ' οσον πλείονα τιμὴν ἔχει τοῦ οἴκου ὁ κατασκευάσας αὐτόν·*

Moses was a mighty man. Moses is the author of the first 5 books of the Old Testament. We know some very unbecoming things about him. He sinned a lot. Oh there it is, he sinned. Moses was just a man. God loved him however. God served justice on Moses too. Jesus was the son of God, or rather God in human form. He lived a holy life on Earth. He never sinned. How could he, he is GOD! There are many mighty men in the Bible but no man mightier than Moses. There is only one mighty and holy man in the Bible, Jesus. God sent his son (aka as himself in human form) to fulfill prophesy, fulfill the law, fulfill everything Moses wrote about. But mostly to save the world because we have all screwed up. You are a sinner. I am a sinner. We were born into a sinful world. (thanks Adam and Eve) but Gods plan was Jesus. Now as sinners, we have a savior.

Prayer**Moses was something else. He lived a passionate life. Anger fueled him in Egypt. Love for God fueled him in the wilderness. Pride fueled him sometimes too. We look to Moses as a testament to one like us but had a love for you like no other. Jesus, your son is all I need. He is greater and sinless. He is my savior for I am a sinner and deserve your wrath. Thank you

Your Thoughts…

Day Seventy-Three

Matthew 28:16-20*Mark 16:15-18*Luke 24:45-49

Matthew--Then the eleven disciples went to Galilee, to the mountain where Jesus had told them to go. When they saw him, they worshiped him; but some doubted. Then Jesus came to them and said, "All authority in heaven and on earth has been given to me. Therefore go and make disciples of all nations, baptizing them in the name of the Father and of the Son and of the Holy Spirit, and teaching them to obey everything I have commanded you. And surely I am with you always, to the very end of the age."

Mark--He said to them, "Go into all the world and preach the gospel to all creation. Whoever believes and is baptized will be saved, but whoever does not believe will be condemned. And these signs will accompany those who believe: In my name they will drive out demons; they will speak in new tongues; they will pick up snakes with their hands; and when they drink deadly poison, it will not hurt them at all; they will place their hands on sick people, and they will get well."

Luke--when he opened their minds so they could understand the Scriptures. He told them, "This is what is written: The Messiah will suffer and rise from the dead on the third day, and repentance for the forgiveness of sins will be preached in his name to all nations, beginning at Jerusalem. You are witnesses of these things. I am going to send you what my Father has promised; but stay in the city until you have been clothed with power from on high."

*Greek**Matthew--Oἱ δὲ ἕνδεκα μαθηταὶ ἐπορεύθησαν εἰς τὴν Γαλιλαίαν εἰς τὸ ὅρος οὗ ἐτάξατο αὐτοῖς ὁ Ἰησοῦς, καὶ ἰδόντες αὐτὸν προσεκύνησαν, οἱ δὲ ἐδίστασαν. καὶ προσελθὼν ὁ Ἰησοῦς ἐλάλησεν αὐτοῖς λέγων, Ἐδόθη μοι πᾶσα ἐξουσία ἐν οὐρανῷ καὶ ἐπὶ [τῆσ] γῆς. πορευθέντες οὖν μαθητεύσατε πάντα τὰ ἔθνη, βαπτίζοντες αὐτοὺς εἰς τὸ ὄνομα τοῦ πατρὸς καὶ τοῦ υἱοῦ καὶ τοῦ ἁγίου πνεύματος, διδάσκοντες αὐτοὺς τηρεῖν πάντα ὅσα ἐνετειλάμην ὑμῖν· καὶ ἰδοὺ ἐγὼ μεθ' ὑμῶν εἰμι πάσας τὰς ἡμέρας ἕως τῆς συντελείας τοῦ αἰῶνος.*

Mark-- καὶ εἶπεν αὐτοῖς, Πορευθέντες εἰς τὸν κόσμον ἅπαντα κηρύξατε τὸ εὐαγγέλιον πάσῃ τῇ κτίσει. ὁ πιστεύσας καὶ βαπτισθεὶς σωθήσεται, ὁ δὲ ἀπιστήσας κατακριθήσεται. σημεῖα δὲ τοῖς πιστεύσασιν ταῦτα παρακολουθήσει· ἐν τῷ ὀνόματί μου δαιμόνια ἐκβαλοῦσιν, γλώσσαις λαλήσουσιν καιναῖς, [καὶ ἐν ταῖς χερσὶν] ὄφεις ἀροῦσιν, κἂν θανάσιμόν τι πίωσιν οὐ μὴ αὐτοὺς βλάψῃ, ἐπὶ ἀρρώστους χεῖρας ἐπιθήσουσιν καὶ καλῶς ἕξουσιν.

Luke-- τότε διήνοιξεν αὐτῶν τὸν νοῦν τοῦ συνιέναι τὰς γραφάς. καὶ εἶπεν αὐτοῖς ὅτι Οὕτως γέγραπται παθεῖν τὸν Χριστὸν καὶ ἀναστῆναι ἐκ νεκρῶν τῇ τρίτῃ ἡμέρᾳ, καὶ κηρυχθῆναι ἐπὶ τῷ ὀνόματι αὐτοῦ μετάνοιαν εἰς ἄφεσιν ἁμαρτιῶν εἰς πάντα τὰ ἔθνη ἀρξάμενοι ἀπὸ Ἱερουσαλήμ· ὑμεῖς μάρτυρες τούτων. καὶ [ἰδοὺ] ἐγὼ ἀποστέλλω τὴν ἐπαγγελίαν τοῦ πατρός μου ἐφ' ὑμᾶς· ὑμεῖς δὲ καθίσατε ἐν τῇ πόλει ἕως οὗ ἐνδύσησθε ἐξ ὕψους δύναμιν.

Today I am not going to prattle on. Today you read and then you do. Go! Share! Encourage! Honor! Love!

Prayer**Send me!

Appendix

The Hebrew Alphabets

ד DALET	ג GIMEL	ב BET	א ALEF
ח CHET	ז ZAYIN	ו VAV	ה HE
ל LAMED	כ KAF	י YOD	ט TET
ע AYIN	ס SAMECH	נ NUN	מ MEM
ר RESH	ק QOF	צ TSADEH	פ PEH
	ת AV	ש SHIN	

The Greek Alphabet

A α	B β	Γ γ	Δ δ	E ε	Z ζ	H η	Θ θ
ἄλφα	βῆτα	γάμμα	δέλτα	ἐψιλόν	ζῆτα	ῆτα	θῆτα
alpha	beta	gamma	delta	epsilon	zeta	eta	theta
a	b	g	d	e	z	ē	th
[aˈa:]	[b]	[g]	[d]	[e]	[zd̠/dz]	[ε:]	[tʰ]

I ι	K κ	Λ λ	M μ	N ν	Ξ ξ	O o	Π π
ἰῶτα	Κάππα	Λάμβδα	μῦ	νῦ	ξεῖ	ὄμικρόν	πεῖ
iota	kappa	lambda	mu	nu	xi	omicron	pi
i	k	l	m	n	ks/x	o	p
[iˈi:]	[k]	[l]	[m]	[n]	[ks]	[o]	[p]

P ρ	Σ σ/ς	T τ	Y υ	Φ φ	X χ	Ψ ψ	Ω ω
ῥῶ	σῖγμα	ταῦ	ὑψιλον	φεῖ	χεῖ	ψεῖ	ὠμέγα
rho	sigma	tau	upsilon	phi	chi	psi	omega
r/rh	s	t	u/y	ph	kh/ch	ps	ō
[r]	[sˈz]	[t]	[yˈy:]	[pʰ]	[kʰ]	[ps]	[ɔ:]

Biblevise

No.	Parables of Jesus	Matthew	Mark	Luke
1	New Cloth and New Wineskins	Matthew 9:16-17	Mark 2:21-22	Luke 5:36-39
2	The Lamp on a Stand	Matthew 5:14-16	Mark 4:21-25	Luke 8:16-18
3	The Wise and the Foolish Builders	Matthew 7:24-27		Luke 6:47-49
4	The Two Debtors			Luke 7:41-43
5	The Rich Fool			Luke 12:16-21
6	The Watchful Servants			Luke 12:35-40
7	The Faithful Servant	Matthew 24:45-51		Luke 12:42-48
8	The Barren Fig Tree			Luke 13:6-9
9	The Sower	Matthew 13:3-23	Mark 4:3-20	Luke 8:5-15
10	The Weeds	Matthew 13:24-30, 36-43		
11	The Growing Seed		Mark 4:26-29	
12	The Mustard Seed	Matthew 13:31-32	Mark 4:30-32	Luke 13:18-19
13	The Yeast	Matthew 13:33		Luke 13:20-21

14	The Hidden Treasure and the Pearl	Matthew 13:44-46		
15	The Net	Matthew 13:47-50		
16	The Householder	Matthew 13:52		
17	The Lost Sheep	Matthew 18:12-14		Luke 15:3-7
18	The Master and Servant			Luke 17:7-10

9 7 9 8 9 0 2 2 4 1 1 7 1